"Our passion for categorization, life neatly fitted into pegs, has led to an unforeseen, paradoxical distress; confusion, a breakdown of meaning. Those categories which were means to define and control the world for us have boomeranged us into chaos; in which limbo we whirl, clutching the straws of our definitions."

~

James Baldwin, *Everybody's Protest Novel*

The Culture Bores

Contents

Introduction

In 1992, Pat Buchanan mounted a run for the Republican nomination for President in a post-Reagan US political landscape. Buchanan was a strongly opinionated conservative commentator and critic of ideologically liberal dissent to the favoritism towards the Reagan era as one of the greatest in American history. Like many American conservatives, there was a growing unrest in the rift between themselves and their liberal peers that expanded their opposition to cooperation as well as broadened their rhetorical attacks of the liberal ideology by-in-large. However, it's what Buchanan said at the 1992 Republican National Convention that sparked a heightened interest in a concept that has since swept American political interest with a deep impact on the perception of ideological opponents to the very means by which voters mobilize themselves to the polls on election day. During his speech supporting George W. Bush after losing to the Jr Bush during the primaries, Buchanan states "There is a religious war going on in our country for the soul of America. It is a cultural war, as critical to the kind of nation we will one day be as was the Cold War itself."[1]

The term "Culture War" became a popular—yet elusive—term to define a set of intellectual and ideological disagreements that have spilled over into policy actions in larger and larger increments since the term was disseminated by Pat Buchanan at the '92

---

[1] Buchanan, "1992 Republican National Convention Speech."

Republican National Convention. Despite how popular it is as far as terminology goes, however, most people cannot even define the phrase. In 2021, Times Radio conducted a poll asking, "When politicians talk about a 'culture war,' what do you think they mean?" 76% simply responded 'I don't know.'[2] This presents a problem in the current political climate, however, when politicians and political movements are rising to prominence upon a foundation of 'culture wars' issues.

Among the most prominent in the political environment who rose to prominence, jumping from Representative to Governor to Presidential Candidate in a mere matter of years, all on the wings of the ill-defined 'culture wars' is Florida Governor Ron DeSantis, who may otherwise be impotent if it weren't for his relevance alongside the culture war issues he has associated himself with. While economic policies that have resulted in record surpluses in the state budget[3] and a new curriculum standard that aimed to eliminate overreliance on testing and introduce concepts across academic disciplines earlier in Florida students' education[4] are fine and dandy, his reputation as a rising star in the politics of the Republican party, which is at the center of the rise of the 'culture wars' according to liberal critics, is the result of his policies regarding them—banning any K-12 educational material that teaches a critical

---

[2] Anthony, "Everything You Wanted to Know about the Culture Wars – but Were Afraid to Ask."

[3] "Governor Ron DeSantis Highlights Administration's Major Accomplishments of 2020."

[4] "Understanding the New Florida B.E.S.T. Standards."

viewpoint through Marxist ideology, any resemblance to critical race theory (teaching the US was systemically built upon an ideology of racism) in schools and businesses to just about any capacity.[5] While a traditional understanding of liberal versus conservative politics would have you believe that the precipice of their divergence was upon "big government" versus "small government," largely hinging upon economic and social interference at the hands of the government as an agent of authority, it immediately dissolves away when observing the means in which popular political figures enact policy along the lines of how government handles issues like the 'culture wars.' This is but one isolated example within an isolated example that displays the issue with the 'culture wars' as a very topic and how it impacts the United States' political discourse. Figures from Bernie Sanders to Donald Trump have increasingly participated in a rhetorical battle involving issues from abortion to whether people say "Merry Christmas," and tout them as a part of their contribution to winning the 'culture wars' once and for all.

But what is this battle, really? And more importantly, what kind of impact does the increasing importance of the 'culture wars' have on voters, materializing in their political habits and attitudes towards dissent. In *The Culture Bores*, I intend to atomize our understanding of the 'culture wars' and increasing reliance on the rhetoric associated with it to argue that these 'culture wars' make no significant

---

[5] "Governor DeSantis Announces Legislative Proposal to Stop W.O.K.E. Activism and Critical Race Theory in Schools and Corporations."

contribution to the national political discourse. In fact, they—and by extension, their increasing importance—are harming such discourse. To demonstrate this perspective, *The Culture Bores* will be broken into three major parts. First, I will attempt to define what a 'culture war' actually is; determining the etymology of a culture war issue, looking for recurring markers of a culture war issue, and the materialization of these attitudes and definitions in some case-specific issues we assign to the 'culture wars' cohort. Second, I will explore how the 'culture wars' are actually won; designing a stratagem of the culture warrior to understand their behaviors and attitudes, exploring the role of aesthetics in the culture wars as a driving force of their existence, and combining these things together to assess the larger issue of 'winning' the culture wars, and understanding how to divide between the material and immaterial parts that make up the culture wars. And third, I will assess the relationship between culture wars rhetoric and policy and attitudes about democracy as a form of government; are the 'culture wars' a dog whistle for authoritarian beliefs about government, does embracing the oft absolute rhetoric of a culture wars issue cause a decline in trust in democracy and basic values such as liberty or justice when they do not bend in a partisan direction, and how partisan factionalism plays a part in all of these issues.

The 'culture wars' have permeated American political, social and (duh) cultural discourse. There is clearly no going back now. However, with prime political figures and entire organized factions with wealth and power to back them banking their political victories on heightening rhetoric that there is a spiritual battle occurring that must be won by their side for anything America stands for to be regained is an alarming development in our political evolution. And in *The Culture Bores* I hope to prove that they're betting on the wrong horse, and endangering American Democracy in the process.

Part I

Defining the Culture Wars

Chapter One
The Etymology of Culture

So much of what we understand today about culture itself lies with the development of anthropology in the nineteenth and twentieth centuries. Piggybacking from Darwin's discoveries on the process of evolution, anthropology—particularly cultural anthropology as it would later become known—would look at the notion of innate biological differences during a time when social commentariats and political actors were using them as justification for ideologies of supremacy and doubting their findings. Most notably, the work of Prussian-born American immigrant Franz Boas, who determined what he called the "plasticity of human types," upsetting long-held beliefs that racial (and what we now call ethnic) differences were immutable and innate.[6]

More than this, Boas also engaged in ethnography, a practice of immersing oneself in the culture or lifestyles of another group outside our own, leaving the biases or setbacks of our own cultural education behind. And what he discovered, as many of his students have since rediscovered, is that instead of finding one lifestyle to be superior in every way to another, each has their own benefits and setbacks that themselves are largely contingent upon that which the

---

[6] Menand, "How Cultural Anthropologists Redefined Humanity."

individual is already exposed to. What many of the early anthropological legends we know of today discovered, from Franz Boas to Zora Neal Hurston, boils down to some key themes: attempting to discover and understand quickly disappearing cultures that hadn't been touched in some way by western influence, to compare our own cultural cohesion to those of opposite cultures, and to question the narrative of cultural supremacy in a world that (as evidenced by the first note in this list) was gradually becoming homogenous. It's from these beginnings, we too, begin our exploration of culture. This chapter will be composed of three major questions: How did once random incongruent social practices become traditions that span generations and continents? How did the rise of "western culture" lend itself to the dominance of these cultural norms and practices? And finally, what are the ways these issues impact our modern understanding of culture as a concept?

The Development of Culture

One of the greatest setbacks in detailing the history of culture is that so much of the discourse surrounding culture—in both academic and political debate circles—is retrospective in nature. While we understand (or have some partial understanding) of the historical trends of the past, we tend to align those complex trends with one or two instantly recognizable events or figures who stand in as the representative for decades of history. However, while cultural history may likely stem from a complex combination of events happening in congruence to or leading into one another, we can pinpoint some theoretical framework and data collected to underscore how culture developed into what we understand it to be today. Returning to the beginning of the chapter, so much of the anthropological research on cultural development stems as far back as Darwinian evolutionary theory. In his 2017 research article, Brian Hare states "Darwin viewed the evolution of human intelligence and morality as the greatest challenge for his theory of evolution through natural selection," and argues that human cognition and psychology are largely due to early cooperative-communication skills and a selection for prosociality, or positively social acts, in *homo sapiens,*[7] otherwise known as the Human Self-Domestication hypothesis (HSD). The reason this matters at all is largely due to the idea that in order to have culture, we must find evidence of cultural artifacts. And what better cultural artifacts are there than the first tools?

Part of the evidence presented by Hare's 2017 article attributes "behavioral modernity," which in short can be described as the establishment of behavioral reasoning and symbolic thought. He claims that "Cieri et al. (2014) explored the possibility that the explosion of cultural artifacts beginning around 80 [thousand years ago] occurred due to selection for temperament that allowed more cooperative communication and promoted rapid transmission of innovations."[8] In short, it's believed that many of what we consider modern human behavioral traits, traits

---

[7] Hare, "Survival of the Friendliest," 156.
[8] Hare, 167.

that we can attribute to the development of our cultural norms and standards, would have taken a few hundred years to develop among tribes of humans. More than this, there's evidence to imply that once that the brains of humans developed to the size that would allow for such behavioral development, a selection for temperament and cooperative communication became evident, thus lending itself to the development of behavioral abilities that would then lead to what Hare describes to be a transition into "the technology revolution of the Upper Paleolithic."[9] This position is supported by Creanza et al. (2017), which looked very briefly at innovation and transmission in cultural evolution. In the section, part of a larger paper attempting to draw a line between genes and cultural traits to explain cultural evolution, they find that, like physical innovations, "new information enters a population via trial-and-error learning or individual interactions with the environment."[10] Their finding expands on Hare's by claiming that it may not only be the development of the human brain that facilitates the behavioral norms that lead to a rise in cultural artifacts such as the burst in tools found in the Upper Paleolithic era, but also the interdependence of cultural innovations leading to cultural equilibrium, especially in the case when such innovations are combined in new ways.

These "cultural innovations" are anything from the burst in artifacts found in the Upper Paleolithic era, allowing cultural developments such as

---

[9] Hare, 167.

[10] Creanza, Kolodny, and Feldman, "Cultural Evolutionary Theory," 7783.

construction and writing to be more available, to new methods of farming, allowing the possibility of feeding more people, thus increasing the population. And like a domino effect, these innovations would have likely played into one another to connect once independent tribes of humans with arbitrary methods of behavioral cohesion to create uniform cultural standards that become the cultural practices and norms we know of today, differentiated only by minor denotations that we might see based on the environmental input that each culture, as the human race overall begins to spread to all corners of the Earth.

On norms, one 2014 review which investigates the emergence of prosociality in toddlers most notably and compares its findings to other animals—namely, primates—looks at the development of our behavioral norms as not just the culmination of cultural innovations or the development of a larger brain and more globular head, but also a form of social conditioning that takes the prior two developments and adds the factor of social conditioning. They quote a line of research that found that by 2-3 years old, toddlers criticize what they called "norm violations," saying that "3-year old children learn novel conventional norms by mere incidental observation of a confident adult that does not perform a game-like action for the child's benefit. Hence, young children are not only adept at following conventional norms, they even enforce them when third parties transgress[.]"[11] This enhances our understanding of cultural development by taking the cultural

---

[11] Jensen, Vaish, and Schmidt, "The Emergence of Human Prosociality," 8.

innovations made as the human mind grew larger and creating a streamlined process through which we would inevitably enforce the standards that result from those innovations. In short, as the human brain evolved to become what it is today, and our species developed the cultural innovations that now define different sects of our societies, we ensured their perpetuity, or at the very least their temporal continuance through our natural ability to perceive, understand and enforce norms at a very young age—no doubt a result of an evolved mind itself. However, this acceptance and enforcement is exclusive to the in-group when concerning conventional norms according to the authors of the 2014 review, supporting the idea that people understand from a young age that the conventional norms of their society or culture are exclusive to those who would be exposed to it, and an exception should be made for those who may not have the same exposure.[12]

And thus, I believe a satisfactory origin of culture is established: Once arbitrary social norms determined on survival instincts turn into cultural developments that gain more in meaning as the human brain grows, and the human being evolves into who we are today, influenced by our biology, our environment, and the cultural innovations we create themselves. Through normative pattern development, a result itself of our brain's evolution, these innovations are accepted and enforced among the in-group, and in a very simple context, culture is born.

---

[12] Jensen, Vaish, and Schmidt, 8.

The Rise and Power of the West

In the context of history, what we've established is that tribes of humans grew and developed, creating artifacts, huts, towns, cities, written word, food and language that evolved in both its form as well as its importance to the cultural cohesion of the tribe, which itself could be labeled the "culture" at this point to encompass the sheer size of these not-so-nomadic groups of humans influenced both by a predisposition for survival and the environment they are born into. However, what catches our attention—as it did the attention of Franz Boas and his contemporaries—is the rise of western culture as an anchor for the rest of the world's cultures to, often against their will, reflect the values and attitudes of this omnipotent entity known solely as "The West."

Much of the rhetoric involved in these cultural debates involving "The West" as an entity start with the Roman Empire. Rome has such a storied history, *literally*. Drawing from her seminal overview of the classical world, Mary Beard writes extensively of the rise of the empire from its pseudo-democratic roots to its historic decline. While the romantic story of Romulus and Remulus raised by a mother wolf entices the patriotism of ancient historians, the possible alternative that Beard paraphrases Livy in detailing in his history of Rome is that this city started as a band of Romulus and his friends. But this would never have lasted on its own. In order to grow at its conception,

Beard presents Livy's explanation that early Rome had to expand its population through a violent motte and bailey. The motte being an unassuming invitation to families and women across the Italian peninsula to come to the city and engage in a religious festival, the bailey being the kidnapping and rape of women lured into Rome by this inticing invitation by its current population, made up of convicts and exiles.[13] But it's not just this violent act that defines Rome's history with the outside world—rather, I believe you'll find it's an entire host of violent acts. Wars, trade disputes, political clashes, domestic acts of dynasty building, and the effort to destroy those dynasties in place of new ones. Simply put, the Roman world, and by extension "The West" as we know it, expanded far and wide because of violent impediments upon the lives and liberties of other, neighboring empires and civil entities that served some kind of purpose or interest to Rome. In Beard's words, "After the Second Punic War, there were regularly more than 30,000 Roman citizens in the army outside Italy, anywhere from Spain to the eastern Mediterranean."[14]

On one hand, I could argue that Rome, the grandfather of western traditions and ideals, set the precedent for the western world's homogeneity. That, even in the face of the collapse of civilization into the dark ages, Rome's ashes left behind a large enough impact that can still be felt to this day. And while, yes, that's half-true, I think rather Rome followed the same example humans have instinctively followed since our species' inception, an example their shadow

---

[13] Beard, *SPQR*, 60.
[14] Beard, 200.

merely relayed as evidence of its durability, rather than innovated in any way. As we established in the previous section, the development of culture comes from a combination of instinctive survival mechanisms turned into invaluable moral authorities within a tribe as the human mind evolved. Human tribalism is a universal, perhaps innate feature of our evolution.[15] It influences how we view other groups in overtly negative ways that can be self-serving.[16] If we combine this with our understanding of Roman imperialism, which can be used as the shorthand for the violence, enslavement and conquering of the western world during their height, we see the history of the world over displayed. Through overtly negative connotations of foreign enemies and exaggerated claims that they were requested as an aid by their allies, the Roman state justifies heightened military presence and prolonged military campaigns across the mediterranean.[17]

This is a familiar story. While Roman imperialism was likely incredibly lax depending on the situation, it has the familiar tint of imperial control that, to this day, academics cite as a source for the layout of the modern world. In Beard's description, "the Romans did not attempt to annex overseas territory systematically or to impose standard mechanisms of control ... The Romans' forms of political control were equally varied, ranging from hands-off treaties of 'friendship', through the taking of hostages as a guarantee of good behaviour,

---

[15] Clark et al., "Tribalism Is Human Nature."
[16] Clark et al., 7.
[17] Beard, *SPQR*, 193.

to the more or less permanent presence of Roman troops and Roman officials."[18] What she describes here is a case-in-point example of the early development of what will soon become colonialism. While what Rome engaged with was never colonial in nature, it sets up the foundations for a kind of world-wide political and economic overreach that later empires, including the British, the Spanish and the United States of America would engage in.[19] Between the proven durability of conquest through (often) violent means left behind by the Roman Empire as the source of "The West" as an entity, and the later colonial acts of western nations across the globe, the power of this entity becomes quite tangible. In layman's terms, "The West" was born out of the forceful spread of ideas from antiquity and the classical era, combining the values of democracy explored in Greece and the imperial dominance of the Roman Empire in an ambivalent mess that would survive the middle ages and influence the British and later the Americans as the dominant representative of this faceless entity. Its dominance, much like its roman and greek ancestors, came too from acts of violence that defined their military and economic power over nations not powerful enough to resist their influence.

---

[18] Beard, 195–96.
[19] Kohn and Reddy, "Colonialism," pt. 1.

Rectifying the Impact of Cultural Dominance

This isn't to say that those subjected to this dominant, forceful presence didn't try to fight back. In many ways, scholars believe they did. From resistance by neighboring states to the Roman Empire's persistent presence, to the American Revolution, to the Sepoy Mutiny in 1857, those groups of people whose cultures, whether based on their politics, race, religion or otherwise, were dominated by this entity known as "The West" have taken up arms—both metaphorically with their words and ideas as well as literally in acts of resistance to this colonial and imperial power. Resistance has also come in the form of cultural amalgamation. Instead of assimilating to the dominant cultural force, in this case "The West," many cultures have quietly merged themselves into the dominant culture's larger cultural cohesion, permanently making a mark on the dominant culture that changes it in ways that preserve the cultural origins of the oppressed group. In the case of America, this could be seen as anything from the music we listen to (Rock n' Roll was invented by Black Americans[20]), to the food we eat (the fascination with foods that native people in the americas ate and vice versa after the columbian exchange[21]). Small acts of resistance that blended the cultural identities of oppressed groups with the larger weave of cultural cohesion that Western powers have had has shaped

---

[20] "Rock and Roll | History, Songs, Artists, & Facts | Britannica."
[21] Mariani, "How Immigrants From Everywhere Made American Food The Most Diverse In The World."

western history in monumental ways, and led to many of the heated cultural debates we see today that exemplify this struggle to understand who, exactly, "The West" really is for centuries.

Now, I think it's appropriate to end this chapter by exploring the issue Franz Boas dedicated a portion of his research to: rectifying this aryan belief that culture was attained—and it was attained through the enforcement of aryan standards, western standards. Instead, Boas found that culture was more of a way of life, and no one culture or its understanding of being human was the definitive article of these cultural descriptions of humanity.[22]

When we talk about the impact of cultural dominance, the discourse often sounds a lot like what we covered in the previous section: imperialism, colonialism, and oppression. Many leftist scholars and activists tie much of the modern industrial world to these overbearing presences, and not for bad reason. As we covered, the rise of the west as a culturally dominant force in the world has a history of force, informed by tribal instincts that, while natural, are quite literally leftovers from a much smaller human brain. But, when you look at the influence of the west on the rest of the world, whether it be the spread of McDonald's or the 2008 invasion of Iraq, how does one exactly *rectify* that? In simple terms, looking back at what has been done already, where do we go from here?

---

[22] Menand, "How Cultural Anthropologists Redefined Humanity," para. 15.

Boas' research always had one goal in mind: to dampen claims of aryan supremacy. To dismiss the idea that "culture" was a level of supremacy that could only be attained through specific developments that white society approved. Instead, he intended to delegitimize these claims through his understanding that culture was this way of life, informed both by the innate biology of the human brain as well as the environmental factors that a person is exposed to. Through this research, Boas and his students attempted to protect the vulnerable cultures of the world from being erased entirely, preserving their sense of independence from this overarching force attempting to force assimilation onto them. Today, we see reflections of this sentiment in the popular discourse on cultural rectification. Black, asian, left-wing, right-wing, indigenous, immigrant, and other cultural factions often debate, fight for and memorialize their respective histories with an intent not to be forgotten. While, in the context of America, cultural amalgamation is still an option at resistance, there is this air that resistance is no longer enough. Activists look to the dominance of the west and these western (and often eurocentric) cultural ideas and attitudes with disdain, with intentions not just to amalgamate with them into a new cultural apparatus, but instead to weaken the dominant force and force it to share the stage with the lesser-known cultural entities it once oppressed.

This strategy is born of pride and anger. Pride in one's cultural heritage; anger towards the world for suppressing it. But the way I see it, a balance must be struck between these cultural divisions in order to progress into the next era of human intellectual evolution. Domination, as the empires of history have proven, is a nonsolution. It leads to the unnecessary suffering of these oppressed cultures based on arbitrary and, as Boas and his students proved, unfounded beliefs of superiority. However, the issue could also become a miscommunication between different cultural factions, should they choose not to behave themselves when having to share the spotlight. As stated before, tribalism is a natural part of human evolution. It could be posited that, in this new age of cultural cohabitation, the "tribes" each of these cultures represent could become embittered having to share spaces with other cultures that don't prescribe to or respect the autonomy of themselves. The sensitive nature of tribal disagreements could become unruly, explosive even, if not perpetually tempered by cooler heads. This then leads to the question: in an increasingly globalized world of deeply rooted cultural schisms, how could we ever possibly build a body of these "cooler heads" that could ensure both the prevention of unjust cultural domination *and* the unnecessary factional violence that could result from cultures not fully equipped for the cohabitational future our species strives towards?

For now, that question may be best left unanswered, as in the age of post-Trump politics, domination and factional violence seem only to be getting worse. And while perhaps a messiah is around the corner coming to fix it all, I think the more accurate answer might be a cooperative effort across cultures to ensure no one among them reaches the violent dominance that is definitive of this new era of politics.

Chapter Two

Signs a Culture War is Afoot

In my mission to define the 'culture wars', I came across one name very frequently: James Davison Hunter. In 1991, when the culture wars were beginning to get their name, Hunter wrote a book that thrusted the term into common discussion and explored the causes and consequences of culture war discourse titled very simply "Culture Wars," that dived into what subjects constituted these wars, largely focusing on a spiritual battle between religious fundamentalists and secularists as a result of thirty years of discourse on issues from abortion to gay rights. In 2021, Hunter joined *Politico* to discuss the expansion of this term, and it's this interview that I feel gives us the most in-depth and concrete foundation to find recurring symbols that what you are discussing is a "culture war" before it is a simple subject like economic policy.

First, Hunter describes a 'culture war' as "a political battle over certain kinds of cultural issues, like abortion, sexuality, family values, church-state issues, and so on. [It's] really about the mobilization of political resources —of people and votes and parties—around certain positions on cultural issues."[23] Hunter expands this with a seemingly contradictory idea that, despite being a political opportunity to rally your movement's votes during an election season, the

---

[23] Stanton, "How the 'Culture War' Could Break Democracy."

'culture wars' are still very much a symbol of how our deeper cultural beliefs impact those politics. "It's really about both things," Hunter told *Politico*.

What Hunter prescribes here is the notion that the 'culture wars' may have, as he had written in his 1991 book, been an opportunity for the GOP to rally voters against the liberal establishment in America from ending the glory of the Reagan era in the US, but that those voters weren't literal pawns, empty-headed and simply taking action blindly because their Republican overlords told them—an important distinction to make in determining what is, and by contrast what is not, a 'culture wars' issue. A very common tactic by both the left and the right in discourse on virtually any subject, but most certainly the culture wars, is to conclude that voters in the other party—not the party bosses but Republican card carriers in your local town—are faceless monsters fighting for evil simply because evil resides within them. But this prescription is grossly exaggerated and, in my experience, has lacked substantial thought behind it. It fails to define what evil could even be in this case that is not some skewed definition with a partisan bias written all over it. Then to claim that every single person, or even a majority of them, simply *are* this way and always have been is a preposterous claim to make, and unfalsifiable in nature. Hunter's claim humanizes people by stating that, yes, some way or another, people build a moral logic around their positions on issues like abortion, gay and trans rights, and in their mind, it is genuinely just and true.

In 2015, researchers Andrew Miles and Stephen Vaisey asked this very question, hoping to determine whether the existence of the culture wars led to moral differences playing a part in political identification, or if it was present in perpetuity. Firstly, they established that previous research had confirmed that "morality does – even must – play an important part in shaping their thoughts, feelings, and behaviors both politically and in general."[24] Supporting this, their research confirms that a decade before there were already researchers finding that people were uniting along "ethnicity, religion, nationalism, gender, and sexual orientation" instead of economics, and that morality has become (or may always has been, the jury is still out on that) an innate primary motivator for human behavior.

But more specifically, their research backs up Hunter's claims of morals acting as a backup processor for political-ideological manifestation. They write, "Although conclusions remain speculative, some evidence indicates that conservatives are more likely to view consistency with divine laws, self-control, and behaving in a 'natural' way as morally praiseworthy," and "For their part, liberals are more likely to view preserving nature, ensuring equal opportunities for all, and preventing the killing of humans as morally important."[25] What this tells us is that, given the theoretical foundation explored in more detail within the study, there is a legitimate moral background that informs people's ideological activism that can't be written off as cronyism or

---

[24] Miles and Vaisey, "Morality and Politics," 253.
[25] Miles and Vaisey, 262.

empty-headed obedience towards an all-powerful political institution trying to get votes. In reality, conservatives and liberals are fully fleshed out people, with actual moral attitudes towards issues like religion, abortion, marriage and education that have been capitalized on by the institutions they helped create in order to establish and expand a secure voting base and increase their political influence.

What we can glean from these insights is this as the first sign of a culture war: deep moral attitudes and the emotional reactions they elicit. When speaking about run of the mill political issues, two civil adults will be more likely, and more than willing, to concede ground in the greater interest of the collective group on the condition of little-to-no oversight in their personal business so long as that business fits the agreed upon ethical standards of the group. But with a culture wars issue, people's attitudes are not anchored on desires for collective progress or universal freedom. Instead, people are driven by an intense passion that their ideological position is aligned with—or is itself—this idea of objective moral truth. Meaning if I am a conservative and I consider myself "pro-life," I am so because that position is informed by some grand illusory truth that dictates the very laws of nature. In this mindset, there can be no dissidence because "the truth" has already been decided (be it by a god or some form of spiritual energy that rules the universe). Doing so is an act of heresy, and must be met with swift punishment in order to dissuade further unrest from potential sympathizers. In the eyes of a culture warrior, however, acts of oppression, destruction and in the most extreme cases, death, are not unjustified. Returning to the previous finding, these acts are wholly justified in the eyes of the beholder as a pursuit towards that moral absolute—if people are suffering in some way because, say, they can't transition and suicide rates go up when we try to convert them, it's because they deserve that suffering. The largest blind spot of culture warriors is, in fact, this first marker of the 'culture wars.' The use of moral absolutism despite the abstract nature of this philosophy and blatant lack of evidence for its existence in any objective sense is historically how all forms of dictators justify suffering under their rule. If someone deserves to hurt, then hurting them is no longer wrong.

And if someone engages with us on one of these issues, there is no reason to employ any kind of empathy or nuance in our discussion, because there is none. There are no complexities in issues like abortion because "the truth" dictates there can't be. Therefore, when someone attempts to introduce altering facts or diverging perspectives, a culture warrior has no reason to genuinely engage with those ideas—they are simply wrong, and it's my job to "fix" their opinion or force them into silence so they don't corrupt the susceptible minds of the "uneducated" masses. What this results in are the hallmark screaming matches and winnerless debates that have defined the 'culture wars' for the last five to ten years. People with strict, and as we will explore later often groundless, ideological positions rooted in the protection of a very exclusive class of society on the grounds that such a class' cultural, political, social and religious beliefs are inherently true, morally absolute and entirely righteous in their existence demean, destroy and demand obedience from other people who feel the exact same way about a different class of society. The resulting stalemate becomes the thesis from which the political establishments these different groups have cultivated can capitalize on during elections to easily activate and mobilize their supporters and potential allies with hopes in increasing political power.

I want to shrink further, however, below the moral background of our political action, to the speech itself. Rhetoric is a powerful linguistic tool to state, persuade others of, and enforce one's ideological goals or an opinion on a subject. However, the 'culture wars' have distinct features to the rhetorical strategy of its warriors that allow it to stand out from its peers in ways we can denote. In the May 2022 edition of *Politics*, James Martin argues that rhetoric has a hermeneutic (that is, concerning the philosophical interpretation) quality in discourse that contributes to "its qualities as an activity of assembling and reassembling the meaning of a situation."[26] He elaborates to say that public speech essentially gets a bad wrap in the popular consciousness, that its reputation is defined by petty battles over positions of power that are "perceived as the immediate flux of events, superficial opinions and disagreements, not statements of enduring significance to be closely deciphered."[27]

---

[26] Martin, "Rhetoric, Discourse and the Hermeneutics of Public Speech," 170.
[27] Martin, 173.

Contrary to this public image, where public debates and the rhetorical tools used to win them are a petty ideological game of tug-of-war, Martin finds that these tools and the goals they set out to accomplish have a significant hermeneutical impact on our understanding of both the past and the future. He writes, "Whereas conventional hermeneutics conceives interpretation largely as a process of retrieval – drawing upon (and so repeating faithfully) traditions of understanding to confront the new – [John] Caputo's radical hermeneutics underscores how the very prospect of the new distorts or transforms inherited traditions from within, altering our sense of being."[28] What Martin conveys is this fearful vision of the power of rhetorical hermeneutics in public speech that uses what he describes as an uncertain future to, in a way, discolor our understanding of the past, fundamentally reshaping our ontological self perception. He supports this argument, too, with the scathingly recent example of COVID-19 discourse following the outbreak of the pandemic, noting "a revival among political leaders of the language of 'war', command, technical expertise and collective [mobilization]."

And it's the rhetoric of the pandemic that I want to pause at and dig deeper into Martin's claim. A 2023 study investigated 270 million tweets from over 2.1 million users in the United States to explore "valuable insights into the dynamics of COVID-19 discussions and assist policymakers in better understanding the emergence of ideological

---

[28] Martin, 180.

divisions."[29] They focused on five core issues users discussed online: the origins of the virus, lockdowns, business closures, wearing masks, virtual education and vaccines, then they split tweets by moral foundation level and user ideology, hoping to distinguish the moral language used by conservative and liberal twitter users surrounding COVID-19. By moral foundation level, the study references the ideological framework that drives political behavior described by Jonathan Haidt in 2012.[30] Rao et al. found that care/harm and authority/subversion were the most frequently discussed moral dimensions by users in their data pool, "with strong symmetry between liberals and conservatives suggesting that both groups are driven by external events."[31] In their findings, Rao et al. sees a partisan difference in the moral language surrounding the pandemic, where conservatives see more vices than virtues, and "while both appealed to subversion, betrayal, and cheating when discussing the origins of COVID-19, liberals focus more on harm."[32] They also found elites used more moral language than non-elites on average across political ideology.[33]

This study confirms what we already know based on our understanding of the culture wars: deep moral attitudes motivate the political activity of the culture warrior. However, what I want to do now is associate the findings in Rao et al. with another study

---

[29] Rao et al., "Pandemic Culture Wars," 1.
[30] Haidt, *The Righteous Mind*.
[31] Rao et al., "Pandemic Culture Wars," 6.
[32] Rao et al., 8.
[33] Rao et al., 9.

to contextualize its relationship with Martin's 2022 paper. Van barr et al. (2023) explores what it calls "uncertainty attitudes" (attitudes that have a particular aversion to all feelings of uncertainty) and how they react to political narratives, more than that, how multiple people with shared political values and a aversion towards uncertainty neurally "synchronize," effectively increasing the partisan attitude and group loyalty.[34] Their findings consisted of three major revelations:

First, they saw "increased neural synchrony … observed among committed partisans on each side of the ideological divide, revealing that sharing strong partisan beliefs—regardless of political affiliation—yield polarized neural encoding of a political stimulus at the time of perception."[35] This shows that these heightened partisan reactions to political content exists across the aisle. Despite the political-ideological tendency to omit oneself from guilt at the hands of partisan misperception, it's more likely than not that both sides engage in this misperception more than they'd like to admit.

Second, "uncertainty-intolerant individuals experienced greater brain-to-brain synchrony with politically like-minded peers and lower synchrony with political opponents." (p. 5) In layman's terms, people with a stronger aversion towards uncertainty as a phenomenon will experience a stronger sense of psychological bonding with a politically congruent

---

[34] Van barr et al.,, "Intolerance of uncertainty modulates brain-to-brain synchrony during politically polarized perception"
[35] Van barr et al., 5.

peer than someone with dissimilar political tendencies.

Lastly, "the neural fingerprint of these uncertainty-modulated polarized perceptions predicted subsequent polarized attitudes outside of the scanner." What Van Barr illustrates with this result is that their team was able to essentially predict the polarized attitudes of their respondents based on the previous findings that those aversive to uncertainty with a partisan perception of the political stimuli they presented.

Together, Van Barr et al. argues that these findings show that "uncertainty attitudes gate the shared neural processing of political narratives with our political allies and opponents, thereby fueling polarized attitude formation about hot-button issues." Our need for certainty becomes part of our undoing when, if that need is strong enough, we use our partisan perception of political content to warp our understanding of that event. But it's what they followed this conclusion up with that makes it relevant to Rao et al.'s relationship to Martin's claim. They write, "Evidence of neural synchrony when passively viewing political topics presented with incendiary language, but not during neutrally worded political narratives, reveals that provocative language shapes the rise of polarized perceptions."[36] This is our smoking gun. If the difference between a more polarized and more mundane reaction to political stimuli is whether or not that stimuli is presented with incendiary language, and Rao et al.'s finding that the

---

[36] Van barr et al., 6.

elite use more moralistic language on average than average people while also confirming the fact that moral attitudes heavily inform political behavior, we can moderately claim that the use of heightened moral language, language such as "The question we're facing is whether in the years ahead, we have more freedom or less freedom. More rights or fewer,"[37] and "As president, we will wage a war on the woke ... we have the opportunity to choose a better path, and to reverse the decline,"[38] is employed explicitly to manipulate those moral backgrounds and increase the effective polarization of its audience under the pretense, such as Martin points out, of an uncertain future.

In short, where the first marker of a culture war issue is the deep (if not even exaggerated) moral attitudes surrounding the issue itself, we can too add the rhetorical tools used in public speech about these issues. Culture wars rhetoric is not merely a means to an end, with the explicit goal of presenting a layout of information and argumentative skills that changes one's opinion. To the culture warrior, rhetoric is a weapon meant to enforce the universal truth of their cultural supremacy in a battleground of ideas. Using an uncertainty of the future, the culture warrior can reshape our recollection of the past, thus shifting the collective ontological self perception of their audience. This exploitation of a fear of the uncertainty that their future represents effectively ignites a psychological emergency alert and polarizes their audience (or at the very least, a chunk of their audience), using the emotional reactions that polarization elicits to

---

[37] *Joe Biden Launches His Campaign For President.*
[38] *I'm Running to Reverse the Decline of Our Nation.*

mobilize them towards the current battle they're trying to win.

And much like the first indicator we exposed in this chapter, this use of rhetoric can be just as dangerous as it is helpful. By virtue of its nature, culture wars rhetoric is exploitative of unbridled fear, untamed hate and unprincipled misunderstanding. It exploits the deep moral feelings we associate with the cultural connections we have and maximizes their influence on our political behavior in ways that may spill over into support for a fascist or political violence. Yet its speakers so carelessly use such exploitative rhetoric willingly, often even knowingly, of the possibly dire consequences it may have. While intentions vary from speaker to speaker, the outcomes become self evident. Deep moral attitudes surrounding ideological relationships we form based often, if not primarily, on arbitrary reflections of our opinions or backgrounds are inherently absurd. They are a rejection of the apparent truth of existence that no one tribe is superior to another. As Franz Boas found in his anthropologic work, these differences don't arise from superiority, but from basic necessity. And yet, instead of using the power of rhetoric to reveal this finding and encourage cooperation, culture warriors have weaponized it into a thing meant to obscure such a finding, delegitimizing the work of Boas and his students and endangering civic discourse with the fiery passion of an angry nation.

Throughout this chapter, I have increasingly used the phrase "culture warrior" as a noun to describe this ambiguous group of people engaging in the practices I have attempted to highlight as indicators of these 'culture wars.' However, this practice is abusive on my end and requires clarification. What, really, defines one of these culture warriors compared to someone who may not fit the description? Well, the answer actually lies in our third indicator of the 'culture wars' themselves. Political identity, as we have partially established throughout the last two chapters, is influenced by a plethora of input factors, including where you're from, the people you're surrounded by in life, and the economic and social circumstances you find yourself in. However, in discourse, there is a deviation that those committed to these 'culture wars' take from normal political discourse that embeds these wars into their self perception.

First, I need to lay the groundwork for ideological self-conceptualization. How does one consider oneself a political character at all, let alone a culture warrior? Then, I will distinguish the two identities by what I believe to be the faint subtleties of their political and conceptual makeup. To start, I briefly want to mention the seminal *The American Voter*, which vaguely looked at this conceptualization through the practical lens of voter behavior in 1960. *The American Voter* primarily distinguishes kinds of voters into four distinct categories; ideologues, groups benefits voters, nature of the times voters, or no issue content voters.[39] While political ideology spans across this account, it was Anthony Downs who noticed that a majority of voters in his time would be what we will call ideologically moderate, and he theorized that this ought to draw the political parties towards moderate

---

[39] Campbell et al., *The American Voter*.

policy positions.[40] It's the process of political socialization, however, that I want to focus on for a moment in our quest to understand why people become the political characters they do.

In order to accomplish this, I turn to Tajfel and Turner's Social Identity Theory. In it, they go beyond the practical application of voting behavior, and examine the psyche of identity and explain it as the "individual's knowledge that he belongs to certain social groups together with some emotional and value significance to him of this group membership,"[41] as Hogg (2016) quotes. He continues, "Social groups, whether large demographic categories or small task oriented teams, provide their members with a shared identity that prescribes and evaluates who they are, what they should believe and how they should behave." Here, we understand a critical element that can be applied to the political socialization of the culture warrior, and the politically engaged overall. Political identities do more than fulfill a practical prerequisite for voters, but they provide and expand an ontological sense of self that is critical to the individual's self perception. This foundation is crucial to my argument, as without that sense of self, no culture warrior is going to spend much time advocating for the issues they claim are at the crux of current political life.

But what are the behaviors within and outside the distinct groups we form that legitimize their

---

[40] Rogers, "Some Methodological Difficulties in Anthony Downs's An Economic Theory of Democracy."
[41] Hogg, "Social Identity Theory," 6.

entitativity (meaning the distinctive features that set it apart as an entity) and define the boundaries of their conflicts with out-groups that don't align with them? Hogg (2016) explores this by arguing that we mentally represent the categories we associate with through "prototypes," or fuzzy interrelated characteristics we, as individuals, associate with the category.[42] He expands on this by saying when a group defines itself (or its opposing out-groups) by these fuzzy characteristics, they become instead "stereotypes". To clarify: these distinctive characteristics that Hogg defines are not written anywhere, or cemented by any legal or spoken authority up for amendment. What makes the social categories we self-assign distinct and legitimate entities is simply the arbitrary agreement of enough of those within a group of that group's general characteristics—for simplicity's sake we will call this phenomenon a form of *collective agreement.*

Social Identity Theory was conceptualized under the larger exploration of group conflict. And where this conflict arises is when what Hogg describes as "Rather than 'seeing' that person as an idiosyncratic individual, you see them through the lens of the prototype of the category you have placed them in—they become *depersonalised* [sic] in terms of the attributes of the prototype."[43] This is what I will call a *collective agreement problem*; if collective agreement is the result of a substantive majority of a group agreeing on the nature of a thing (whether that thing be themselves, their society, etc), then what happens when different (perhaps opposing) groups'

---

[42] Hogg, 8.
[43] Hogg, 9.

definitions and boundaries come into conflict with one another? As Hogg (2016) notes, we apply our prototypes in order to best understand how and why someone may affiliate and behave along the lines of an out-group's rules and expectations, and end up not seeing the more universal, three-dimensional makeup of human behavior and instead boil one another down to a few recognizable stereotypes. This breakdown of inconsistent collective agreement should sound familiar, as it's the foundation for the very logic applied by anthropologists and the population at large for hundreds of years, inspiring the aryan supremacy myth that Franz Boas and his students worked to dismantle. Hogg (2016) elaborates that this "simplification" of the character and predicted behavior of out-groups can apply to in-group self perception as well. "Categorisation-based depersonalisation affects in-group members and yourself in exactly the same way. When you categorise [sic] yourself, you view yourself in terms of the defining attributes of the ingroup (self-stereotyping), and since prototypes also describe and prescribe group appropriate ways to think, feel, and behave, you think, feel, and behave group prototypically."[44] This description and the context it's been provided in are massively important in understanding self perception and the development of a "culture warrior" identity.

This importance stems from the establishment of a "culture warrior" mentality in the context of conflict and its relationship to self perception. Using my collective agreement problem framework as an example, if the social identity of various cultural

---

[44] Hogg, 9.

groups, which self-define along arbitrary and fuzzy lines, come into contact, the way they treat each other is heavily dependent on Hogg's application of social identity theory in the context of conflict. In my analysis, a culture warrior internalizes the stereotypes of their cultural in-groups and out-groups as a reflection of the true character and behavior motivations of those groups, respectively. More than this, the culture warrior aligns a particular moral element to their group stereotypes. This is explored, too, under social identity theory, which Hogg says "groups and their members go to great lengths to protect or promote their belief that 'we' are better than 'them'."[45] This stems from a long standing discussion on self-esteem and intergroup relations that typically has found that self-esteem plays some relationship in the individual's perception of their groups and those groups' opponents in a moral context. As Hogg (2016) mentions, however, this discussion can cause some confusion, as results vary on the impact, and perhaps more importantly the direction of impact, between self-esteem and intergroup relations broadly. For our purposes, we'll generally claim that self-esteem and intergroup perceptions play a cyclical, co-symbiotic relationship to one another that provide the human need for a sense of purpose by defining "us" as right and good and "them" as wrong and evil, in the broadest description. Hogg supports this claim in saying "Uncertainty makes it difficult to predict and plan behaviour [sic] in such a way as to be able to act efficaciously ... Ultimately, people need to know who

---

[45] Hogg, 9.

they are, how to behave, and what to think, and who others are, how they might behave, and what they might think."[46]

Hogg's note touches on a point we established earlier via Van Barr et al.'s work in finding uncertainty-averse individuals will "synchronize" with like-minded political peers, particularly when subjected to incendiary political language. Hogg actually explains why this phenomenon occurs when he says "Social categorisation is particularly effective at reducing uncertainty because it furnishes group prototypes that describe how people (including self) will and ought to behave and interact with one another."[47] He expands this point to say that these prototypes tend to be consensual (think in terms of my "collective agreement" framework), thus our worldviews and self perception remain intact.

The development of a "culture warrior" identity relies on a convergence of factors, from a strong aversion to uncertainty, to a strong sense of self-esteem that acts as the culture warrior's combatant to such uncertainty. Their sense of self comes from not only the group they affiliate with, but the rightness and goodness of that group being affirmed when in conflict with alternative ideological factions. This is in part what creates a collective agreement problem. When a society becomes so all encompassing, as perhaps we can postulate America has, that it causes contradictory ideological factions to inhabit the same space, a collective agreement

---

[46] Hogg, 10.
[47] Hogg, 10.

problem emerges where these groups attempt to cross-communicate their understandings of self and society. When the other side doesn't concede to our superior ontology, I believe this "culture warrior" identity emerges, particularly in the most uncertainty-averse and self-esteemed individuals who represent our factions. This is why you may note the majority of culture warriors are politicians or activists. Hogg (2016) explores this in the social identity theory of leadership, saying "In groups, people are highly vigilant for and attentive to reliable information about the context-appropriate group prototype/norm. Typically, the most immediate and reliable source of this information is identity-consistent behaviour [sic] of those members who are generally considered to be most prototypical of the group."[48] By displaying the most prototypical behavior of their group, certain individuals become a case-in-point of the group itself, directing the attention of insiders on how they ought to behave and from outsiders on their poor behavior. More than this, Hogg (2016) also mentions the normative entrepreneurship these prototype leaders are afforded due to the expectation that they are acting in the group's benefit, causing them to be able to diverge from the prototype agreed upon by the group and instead forge a slightly new path for them to follow.

With the context of Hogg's notes on social identity and its role in leadership in particular, and Van barr's research involving aversiveness to uncertainty, I believe we have a stronger understanding of what, or perhaps who, the "culture

---

[48] Hogg, 11.

warrior" really is. Much like in our discussion of the rhetoric of the culture wars, it starts with a strong aversion to uncertainty. When primed, that uncertainty evolves into a strong partisanship that materializes itself by strengthening the prototypical normative behavior within the person and their group. Whether that prototype is to be a pro-life christian nationalist conservative Republican or to be an antifascist pro-choice queer intersectional feminist is less of the point. Our evidence has found that behavioral conditioning towards the group prototype and a partisan adoption of that identity when egged on (at least by incendiary language) is a universal phenomenon. And it's what I think evolves your run-of-the-mill liberal or conservative political activist into a culture warrior. Fear of the uncertainty that conflicting viewpoints represents gives birth to a kind of political character that ceases to simply see themselves as right within a vacuum, but to need to enforce it within their group and against enemies outside. They become prototypical leaders who guide the behavior of their tribe, ironically affording them room for normative entrepreneurship. "The culture warrior" is born of their circumstances. And if the circumstances of their politics becomes adversarial, and they fear the relativity that allowing their adversaries to postulate their own cultural proclivities represents, then they become, one; more attached to their inception of their identity, and two; more willing to fight for it, or enforce it so as not to have to deal with the fear and uncertainty not doing so may represent.

This is a perfect seg-way into the fourth and final indicator of the 'culture wars' I have determined. Put simply, it is an unambiguous disinterest in co-partisan cooperation. This determinant is moreso the marriage of the prior three than it is derived from some external force, but it manifests itself distinctly from the other markers of a culture war to the effect that it's the most visible, in my view. That said, I will introduce some new information that signifies this determinant on its own to clarify the outcomes. I also want to clarify that by 'disinterest in co-partisan cooperation,' I mean to say that both materially, in the form of legislative and electoral politics, and conceptually, in the form of discourse and ideological politics. When exposed for a period of time, the ability of individuals to concede their myths for realities that may include ideological components they don't approve of is diminished into nonexistence.

The conceptualization of an unambiguous disinterest in co-partisan cooperation has, to some degree, already been established by the previous section. However, let's remove it from the baggage of contextualizing it as the result of the development of a kind of character, and instead investigate it as it exists itself. Cooperation is preceded by perception. The likelihood you'll cooperate with someone relies on how you perceive them. And in America today, the two major parties have increasingly unfavorable views of one another. From a Pew report published in September of 2023, it's said that members of either party, and those who more significantly lean towards either party, are more likely to view it in positive terms. It says they view their party as "respectful of democracy, governing honestly and tolerant of different kinds of people. Far fewer say these traits characterize the other party."[49] Furthermore, where members of both parties see themselves overtly positively, they also see the other party overtly negatively, rating the same questions on ethical leadership and policies that interfere with people's lives in an almost mirror fashion. This tracks with our established understanding of social identity theory and the 'culture wars.' The need to be real and impactful becomes a need to be right and good, which necessitates then the need for all others to be wrong and evil.

This is further supported, and begins to allow us to see the 'material' side of disinterest in co-partisan cooperation, by Graham and Svolik (2020), which explored the partisan nature of support for democratic principles by putting its participants through a hypothetical election scenario. They find, "A candidate who considers adopting an undemocratic position can expect to be punished by losing only about 11.7% of his overall vote share. When we restrict attention to candidate-choice scenarios with combinations of partisanship and policies that we typically see in real-world elections, this punishment drops to 3.5%."[50] And the cost of safeguarding democracy in an electoral setting comes at a highly partisan price, as well. They found that only 13.1% of their respondents were willing to defect from voting along their partisan proclivities if it meant supporting a "more" democratic candidate, to use the term (p.

---

[49] "Pew Research Center," para. 10.
[50] Graham and Svolik, "Democracy in America?," 393.

393). Moreover, members in both parties were found to employ a "partisan 'double standard'" against the other side, making them more likely to punish a candidate in the other party for anti/un-democratic behavior than someone in their own party (p. 393). A legitimate concern might be voter education: perhaps this pool of respondents incorrectly distinguished democratic and undemocratic behavior, and thus employed partisan preferentialism as a placeholder. But they considered this, and found that "The vast majority of our respondents correctly distinguish real-world undemocratic practices—including those endorsed by our experimental candidates—from those that are consistent with democratic principles." (p. 393) These findings, they contextualize, are conditional to what we might see as the *strength* of a person's partisanship, as independent "leaners" were found to defect from undemocratic members of their preferred party in a significant enough way to actually defeat them in an electoral setting, while "a majority of strong partisans would rather elect a candidate who violates democratic principles than cross party lines."[51] They found this to be true in co-partisan primary settings as well (p. 400).

These findings elaborate on an understanding of 'conceptual' disinterest in co-partisan cooperation by showing the effects of developing a strong partisan identity in accordance with what we know about social identity theory. Partisan political identity can be seen as a form of insulation from the terror of a subjective and uncertain existence, one that history and sociology has shown we employ to protect ourselves

---

[51] Graham and Svolik, 400.

both from the threat of a potential outside harm as well as from the existential harm of a weak/poor self-perception. Again, that fundamental need to realize ourselves and empower our efficacy in various senses, let alone politically, has led to the historical evolutionary development of political identification that, fairly arbitrarily, constructs itself around moral clarity and intellectual supremacy. I am right and good. Everyone else is wrong and evil. This informs, then, the more 'material' disinterest in co-partisan cooperation. We don't merely see others as wrong and evil in an academic or intellectual setting. We may, as Graham and Svolik (2020) have explored to a degree, be unwilling to punish elected officials or candidates for positions of power who clearly embody anti-democratic principles simply by virtue of their association with the group we share. This may be because to do so then violates the moral and intellectual integrity of the group as a whole. By acknowledging the more violent or dangerous political undertones within our preferred partisan camps, we then must become critical of the camp as a whole, which in and of itself defeats the evolutionary purpose of the camp: to *not* exist with such a degree of moral uncertainty. It causes us, too, to question ourselves if we punish those who align with us all too willing to violate democratic principles to achieve our shared goals. We may think to ourselves "how could I, a good person with true beliefs, have not stopped someone so clearly against the democratic values I (at least in this case, we assume) care for and believe in?" The existential self-doubt it creates in us, again, defies the very reason we form and associate with our groups to begin with, therefore it must be avoided at all costs.

To further understand the 'material' disinterest in co-partisan cooperation, we must first return to themes of the last section of this chapter and revisit their implications. Revisiting his exploration of realistic conflict theory, Michael Hogg (2016) explores how many individual goals are mutually exclusive, which may result in conflict as one person must achieve it and an other must not.[52] He expounds on this to claim, similarly, conflict arises when a goal of two or more groups of people is mutually exclusive as well. He states, "This is often accompanied by destructive intergroup behaviour [sic] and derogatory intergroup attitudes—the foundations of prejudice and discrimination and ultimately dehumanisation [sic]." (p. 5) The behaviors of the 'culture warrior' mentality that we discussed in the previous section become the *norm* adopted by the group as a whole following the lead of a few normative entrepreneurs. We see this play out materially in the makeup, for one, of America's most prominent political parties. Timothy Conlan explores the shift from decentralized national party systems to strong and centralized national systems and their consequences. Conlan (2017) states that "As late as 1964, the national party committees were portrayed as arenas of 'politics without power,' since the real power in both presidential and congressional nominations and election lay with strong state and local party leaders and organizations."[53] However, this relationship has effectively swapped sides since the era of the 1960s, with state and local party apparatus' dissipating while

---

[52] Hogg, "Social Identity Theory," 5.
[53] Conlan, "The Changing Politics of American Federalism," 171.

the national party structures grow stronger both in financial power and political influence. Conlan (2017) finds "Elections for state and local offices are now often fought over national issues like marriage equality and health care ... In the 2017 state elections in Virginia and New Jersey, for example, Democratic candidate ads are emphasizing opposition to Donald Trump and positions on national health insurance policies, in addition to state specific issues."[54] This shift has rippling effects on both national and local politics, insofar as local politics has effectively *become* national with local denotations that take a backseat to the party-picked issues to campaign on and against.

One such influence is the legislative track records of members of congress in both parties increasingly voting *against* their constituent's intuitive economic interests when voting on contentious national policy issues.[55] Where Conlan (2017) argues state and local governments retain their traditional role as laboratories of policy, he states they also quickly lose their leading role when a policy innovation seems to be effective, as national government quickly brings it up the agenda and takes the lead instead. He also reiterates the partisan attitude exacerbation we expect with this sort of development to occur, finding that both liberals and conservatives sort themselves into distinct groups online and in real life, stating "Structurally, the two major political parties have also become more ideologically distinctive and extreme."[56] And while

---

[54] Conlan, 172.
[55] Conlan, 173.
[56] Conlan, 174.

this creates a new norm of stalemates and gridlock in policy, a system of what Conlan calls "conditional party government" has accomplished an array of policy feats on both the national and state levels. As the name implies, these policy feats are conditional to the majority party, and as recent decades have shown will imply a degree of policy instability. Conlan (2017) notes, "As Members of Congress become more intensely partisan and ideologically extreme, a shift in majority control of the institution can lead to dramatic shifts in policy outputs, as each side reverses the policy accomplishments of the other."[57] This has obvious negative side effects that make the ability to engage in political life in America an unsafe bargain as the period to which a law persists may be for a single term or two at best, if legal action isn't taken to deem it unconstitutional by the other side. Even the once unstoppable gubernatorial lobby, Conlan states, is a victim to this party-centered voting trend. He finds "Democratic and Republican governors so often go their separate ways that the NGA is forced to tiptoe around many critical issues of intergovernmental policy." (p. 175)

While Conlan's (2017) focus was the centralization of power, I believe his notes on partisanship qualify our observations on a 'material' disinterest in co-partisan cooperation. Where it might be easy to say that our divisions are overblown or don't exist, these concrete actions that have centralized electoral behavior in such a way that legislator's act against their constituent's interests and once gargantuan lobbies crumble to the partisan

---

[57] Conlan, 175.

battles they now represent is a sign that such division does have a degree of realness to it worth exploring. Santoso et. al. (2023) further qualifies this claim by finding that "perceptions reflect the recent record of cooperative and conflictual events that make up the day-to-day interactions between parties as reported in the media."[58] I believe this research shows that there is, in fact, this 'material' influence of the culture wars on policy in the US, and that this influence can be just as damaging as it may, at times, be useful to some.

What these points clarify for us is that the materialization of our conceptual disinterest in co-partisan cooperation is not merely exaggerated or mythicized. While some good-natured people may claim that our divisions are manufactured or that our behaviors against the "other" side are not fully real, that simply isn't the case. Just how we conceive of ourselves and the world very strictly when engaging with 'the culture wars,' so too may we behave (vote, organize, lobby, etc) in ways that reflect that divided nature. One final time, as I have stressed the majority of this chapter, an evolutionary need has become something else. Something amorphous from its original inception and instead has become a serious issue of monstrous proportions. And it is reflected both in our attitudes about ourselves, the world and the way we interact with it.

This brings us to the end of our notes on the signs of the 'culture wars.' While generalized and in

---

[58] Santoso, Stevenson, and Weschle, "What Drives Perceptions of Partisan Cooperation?," 8.

need of further exploration, I believe these issues can reliably indicate both when the 'culture wars' are the issue truly at hand compared to real policy issues as well as their origins and nature, to a degree. It's worth mentioning here that I do not believe, or perhaps rather I cannot say whether I think all of these signs must be occurring in order to properly denote a culture wars issue or if one of them occurs very intensely alone can do the trick. This epistemology of cultural fighting is at best crude and approximate, and at worst arbitrary and made-up. However, I believe the evidence I have presented has at least made it a possibility that these four determinants can help approach the challenge of recognizing the 'culture wars' in a time when they have become so forward in the political agenda that they practically consume all other issues under their umbrella. Before we continue, let's review the signs of a 'culture wars' issue in brief:

1. Deep moral attitudes and the emotional reactions they elicit.

2. Exploitative rhetoric meant to draw out aforementioned moral attitudes and emotional reactions from an audience.

3. A distinct identity formed around the cultural issue (or "war") one is fighting for/against.

4. An unambiguous disinterest in co-partisan cooperation, in both a 'conceptual' and 'material' sense, often following one after the other.

Chapter Three

The Culture Wars in Action

So far, the first part of this book has aimed at defining the culture wars generally. Having established a general history and theoretical framework to understand them with, I hope to do two things with this final chapter. First, I hope to put my determinants of the culture wars to the test to see if the details we made note of theoretically in chapter two will materialize themselves here, and are replicable. This will determine if any further analysis is accurate, and more importantly, if my understanding of the culture wars is legitimate or not. Second, with a concrete understanding of the culture wars based on the parameters and history I laid out in chapters one and two, we will be more strongly suited to determine the parameters of "winning" them, if one can at all, and their real impact on the people who become the most involved in them and beyond—more to come in parts two and three. Because of the previous reasons, I will also no longer use quotes to talk about the culture wars. If my parameters hold up, then they have transcended the realm of theoretical discussion and become a much more material thing we can discuss and interpret.

While I believe we have begun to transcend our theoretical foundations, we are still in an experimental phase. Therefore, we need to apply them to case-specific issues as a way to test their validity.

Culture wars issues, unlike any other issue in politics, tend not to be defined by one or two primary ideas. Rather, they are the culmination of a collection of values that diverge between individuals, thus creating the "war" aspect in question. Therefore, the examples I have elected to draw from are not necessarily one particular issue, but two or more that become intertwined through the process of culture war-ification. Through the next 4 examples, we will explore my theoretical framework for understanding the culture wars in a clearer sense, and attempt to use it to ascribe these issues under the banner of the culture wars definitionally.

Issue 1: Masterpiece Cakeshop and the Freedom of Speech and Religion

In July of 2012, three years before the landmark Supreme Court decision in *Obergefell v. Hodges* (2015) that found same-sex marriages protected by the law, Charlie Craig and David Mullins got married in Colorado. Wanting to celebrate the wedding with a cake, as is tradition in the US, they approached Masterpiece Cakeshop, owned by Jack Phillips about having a cake made for their union. Phillips, a devout Christian, denied their request on grounds that their request violated his religious convictions[59]. He did offer to sell them any of his premade cakes, but not to customize one that celebrated same-sex marriage.

As a matter of fact, Masterpiece Cakeshop was said to have an explicit policy against these kinds of services—services that violated the religious principles

---

[59] Chemerinsky, "Not a Masterpiece," para. 5.

its owner and its staff held firmly to be true.[60] Their argument held that the first amendment of the American constitution, which protects the freedom of speech and of religion as well as the prohibition on state-sponsored religion. While Colorado's state law prohibited this kind of discrimination, what Phillips did was protest through his business' policy, finding security in the national constitution *over* the state law. Craig and Mullins filed suit against Phillips and Masterpiece Cakeshop in 2012, with the State's Civil Rights Commission opening an investigation and finding Phillips' practice violated the law.[61] This decision was upheld by the state's Court of Appeals and denied for review by the Colorado Supreme Court. The case was eventually heard before the Supreme Court in 2018, where it was ruled in a 7-2 decision to reverse the Colorado Civil Rights Commission's ruling,[62] Justice Athony Kennedy arguing for the majority that they had "elements of a clear and impermissible hostility toward the sincere religious beliefs that motivated his objection." (para. 11)

To better understand to what degree this issue might fall under our theoretical framework of the culture wars, let's begin at the first determinant: are there any deep moral attitudes and strong correlated emotions in this case materialized in their debate? In investigating this case so many years removed, I found two things to be simultaneously true. Jack

---

[60] "Masterpiece Cakeshop v. Colorado Civil Rights Commission - FAQ," para. 3.

[61] Chemerinsky, "Not a Masterpiece," para. 8.

[62] Chemerinsky, para. 6.

Phillips is not a particularly angry man. In fact, he's rather quiet and cordial. But this does not mean he isn't motivated by deep moral attitudes. As a matter of fact, I believe his conviction, and the vivaciousness he is willing to maintain that conviction in all circumstances is evidence of such deep morals. In an interview with ABC, Phillips says "... not about hate, this is about not creating a message and a government forcing me to."[63] This is a message he continued throughout his legal and larger social fight. That the agencies working against him were an act of oppressive government tyrannizing his religious free expression through the art of his cakes, and that his business as extension of his own creative endeavors could not be stifled. While the explicit messaging, and the tone he used to defend it, was cordial in nature, it is still deeply moral and excited the emotions of both Craig and Mullins and those that supported them.

Speaking of Phillips' tone, does the rhetoric used by both sides of this argument exploit the moral divisions in this issue of free speech and religion and fair treatment of consumers in America? Let's consult the experts on the subject, the Alliance Defending Freedom, the conservative legal group that defended Phillips and the ACLU, who acted on behalf of Craig and Mullins. The ADF opens their summary of Phllips' case relatively accurately. They close it, then with the claim "the Commission [gave] a free pass to three different bakers who refused orders from customers opposing same-sex marriage."[64] This

---

[63] *SCOTUS Same-Sex Wedding Cake Decision.*

[64] "Masterpiece Cakeshop v. Colorado Civil Rights Commission," para. 1.

language, whether or not it's true, is certainly evocative. But it's not necessarily exploitative. It taps into feelings of hypocrisy on the part of the Civil Rights Commission, but does not necessarily take heart at the issue of free speech and religion over the right of a gay couple to have the business of Phillips. This comes in paragraph two, where the ADF says more explicitly "the government cannot force artists to use their expressive talents to celebrate events or express ideas that they do not support," and "the government was wrong to punish Jack for peacefully living out his beliefs in the marketplace." (Alliance Defending Freedom, para. 2) It's this framing of the issue, I believe, that is more exploitative of the moral attitudes supporters of Phillips will have about the subject and aims to bring out their attitudes. This rhetoric, of government force where it doesn't belong and the squashing of religious practice in society is reflected in their various interviews and ads for Jack as well.

On the part of the ACLU, their summary frames the law that the Colorado Civil Rights Commission said Masterpiece Cakeshop violated "ensures that people are free to go about their day-to-day lives without worrying they will be turned away from stores, banks, hotels and other public places simply because of who they are."[65] It goes so far to describe Jack's claim that he had a right to refuse to make the cake as a "right to discriminate in violation of Colorado law." (para. 3) Similarly to the ADF, the ACLU effectively frames the issue with the deep moral

---

[65] "Masterpiece Cakeshop v. Colorado Civil Rights Commission - FAQ," para. 2.

attitudes supporters of Craig and Mullins will feel in hopes of drawing it out for the Supreme Court. While the SCOTUS is not a public-facing body, it is often under public scrutiny, and the ACLU knows that mobilizing supporters of Craig and Mullins by framing this issue as a moral maleficence that could endanger future protections for LGBTQ+ and marginalized consumers, by arguing the Supreme Court's decision against them could give more business a license to intentionally discriminate. In the case of the ACLU, it does expressly what James Martin denoted as exploiting a fear of the future to mobilize activists in the present. Even after the case, the ACLU can capitalize on this language to engage further activism against any further decisions such as this.

So far, we have two distinct signals of a culture war for the issue of Masterpiece Cakeshop and the expression of religion in the market, allowing businesses to turn away customers whose request defiles the business' personal practices of morality and culture. What of marker number 3, a distinct identity in the "war" of religious freedom and consumer protection? I believe we will have a harder time arguing this point. As stated before, Jack Phillips isn't a particularly animated man. While his morals deeply motivate his conviction *not* to create a custom wedding cake celebrating a gay wedding, he still sells to LGBTQ+ couples from his pre-made collection. Moreso, separated five years from the Supreme Court's 2018 decision in 2024, Masterpiece Cakeshop's website does not necessarily wear its role in the decision and the further implications it had in politics in America as a badge of honor. On the section where you can view wedding cakes, it does read at the top "Masterpiece Cakeshop is not currently accepting requests to create custom wedding cakes. Please check back in the future,"[66] referring to a policy the store started in defiance of the Judge involved in the original case against Masterpiece Cakeshop's ruling that he had to re-train all of his employees to make cakes for weddings now including same-sex couples.[67] As a matter of fact, activists on both sides may have been animated by their deep morals on either side of the issue, but besides signs with clever slogans for court dates meant to pressure the court of public opinion in their favor, neither side truly incorporated their activism in this issue or the outcome of it years later as a part of who they saw themselves as. Their animation, in short, was limited and concentrated in certain regards to the discussion surrounding it, and didn't linger beyond those concentrations.

Finally, I think we can reasonably argue the nature of this case leans towards the disinterest in co-partisan cooperation as being apparent, to a degree. As far as the material of the case, the issue lies in whether or not Jack Phillips, and his business broadly, can publicly practice their religious convictions by refusing a portion of their services, being making a custom wedding cake, for a couple that violates those convictions.

To deviate for a moment, I need to address the fact that the ADF and Jack's framing of the issue tried to separate the act of the business performing a

---

[66] "Wedding | MASTERPIECE CAKESHOP."
[67] *SCOTUS Same-Sex Wedding Cake Decision.*

service for the couple, thus reducing the scope of the impact by making it appear as if Jack's refusal was a form of artistic expression. I think we can reasonably say that this is not necessarily the same as a private personal interest preserving itself from outside tyranny. As a matter of fact, the ADF's description of the case as "living out [Jack's] belief in the marketplace," (Alliance Defending Freedom, para. 2) is a contradiction of the service that custom wedding cake making is on the part of Masterpiece. It is still in some way a service the business is practicing for the customers. So the question, which the SCOTUS failed to truly address in their 2018 ruling, is really about whether the business can refuse to perform that specific service for the couple.

Returning to the material issue of the case, there is a clear disinterest in cooperation. How can you cooperate in this scenario? Our distinction of material and conceptual disinterest is vital in this understanding. Materially, to 'cooperate,' the court would have to complicate the ability of Jack's business—of all businesses—to perform certain services over others if they violate their personal convictions. In a way, it sort of did. It allowed Jack to say he won't make a cake celebrating a gay wedding, but simultaneously argued the importance of nondiscrimination in the market. For instance, it did not give Jack a right to refuse all service to gay couples. He can't tell gay couples they aren't allowed to shop at Masterpiece Cakeshop at all. This is where conceptual disinterest appears. Those who view Jack's actions and defense of them as "despicable pieces of rhetoric,"[68] as the Colorado Civil Rights Commission argued, must to some degree now accept that Jack refuses to acknowledge the marriage of LGBTQ+ couples the same way he does same-sex couples. In a way, the material and conceptual disinterest in co-partisan cooperation is inexplicably intertwined here. One inherently influences the other, Jack's conceptual disinterest in cooperating with the couple *materializing* in his refusal to make their cake. Yet, even then, while Jack maintains his refusal to make custom wedding cakes for these couples, he still says his business is open to LGBTQ+ patrons in all other avenues consistent with American federal antidiscrimination laws. This softens the degree that his disinterest is apparent, and complicates our understanding of it in context of determining how much of a culture war this issue is, as are its implications.

In our exploration of Masterpiece Cakeshop's battle for freedom of speech and religion versus nondiscrimination in business in America, I hope to have elucidated a few key points. First, I believe we have affirmed the viability of my theoretical framework for understanding the culture wars. We noted ¾ of the markers I clarified in chapter two with relative ease. Second, rather unfortunately for us, we have discovered something new about this framework that requires our further investigation of it in practice. It appears that each marker came with a degree of variability or strength. While Jack wasn't particularly animated, he was deeply morally motivated and the ADF used strong, though not existentially strong

---

[68] *SCOTUS Same-Sex Wedding Cake Decision.*

exploitative rhetoric to extract support from ardent allies in Jack's case. This degree of strength in my framework implies something wholly different about it than I have been implying throughout part one of this book. Rather than conceptualizing these markers as signs that makes something "a culture war," a singular object that belongs to this cohort of political discourse that can be distincted and defined separately from other discourse, we have some evidence to say that all general political discourse may have degrees of variable markers that an issue is *more or less* of a culture war than other issues are. In our next few case explorations, I want to highlight and expand this idea so we have a stronger understanding of how it changes the way we view the culture wars as a general subject, and more importantly for the purposes of part one of this book how to define them on an individual basis.

Issue 2: Trans Rights and Representation in Public Sports

Like any other sport, competitive swimming is tough. But for Lia Thomas, the University of Pennsylvania swimmer who transitioned from her male gender identity to female in 2019[69] and joined the women's swim team accordingly in 2022, it was more so because of the conversations happening *outside* the pool room than in it. Thomas' transition, and her participation in the women's league, sparked a flurry of discourse around competitive advantages to being trans in sports, bubbling up to the point of US

---

[69] Levenson, "How an Ivy League Swimmer Became the Face of the Debate on Transgender Women in Sports," para. 25.

State governments passing bans on transgender teenagers from participating in sports categories that didn't align with their sex at birth. This debate, and the larger transgender inclusion issue of American society today has perplexed and haunted the afterthought of the American popular consciousness.

For our purposes, we'll be exploring if the trans inclusion in public sports debate is a culture war, and not other parts of the larger lexicon that is transgender acceptance and inclusion in America. Let's take the theoretical framework, and the degrees to which it may vary, into account. To what degree does there appear to be a deep moral attitude and emotions surrounding it involved in this issue? For one, Republican senate candidate Vicky Hartzler capitalized on the issue for a campaign ad, saying support for Thomas "destroys women's sports."[70] Nikki Haley, one of the Republican candidates for President in 2023, had said "The idea that we have biological boys playing in girls' sports, it is the women's issue of our time."[71] At least on the side of the opposition, there is a clear inference of deep moral attitudes—of disgust, quite frankly, to this issue. However, we need not rely on inference after all. According to 2022 Gallup polling data, the percent of people who felt that "birth gender," what I would feel is more accurately described as biological sex, should in fact determine the role to which transgender people play in sports participation, 69% compared to 2021's

---

[70] *Coach.*

[71] Migdon, "Haley Calls Transgender Athletes in Sports 'the Women's Issue of Our Time,'" para. 2.

62%.[72] Most concrete of their evidence however, is the pure fact that they found that 55% of their respondents felt that "changing one's gender" was "morally wrong."[73] The evidence is clear, among the American public the issue of transgender people playing sports is a deeply moral one, let alone the individual's choice to transition.

What then, of the rhetoric? I feel Vicky Hartzler and Nikki Haley have demonstrated, to some degree, proof that rhetoric is being used to exploit the moral feelings of those in their base of support. They both harken to a similar message: the idea that transgender women playing in women's league's are, in reality, "men pretending to be women,"[74] effectively invading the sport with the nefarious plot to break all the world records in women's sports so that "real" women never will. My sarcasm aside, this kind of rhetoric requires no deeper exploration than we have already done. By its nature, the conservative discourse on transgender people, let alone their participation in sports or use of bathrooms, is designed to ignite a fire in the hearts of both supporters and detractors of the trans movement. It denies the existence of transgender women as legitimate, always referring to them rather derogatorily as men pretending or biological boys. It then takes this image of a man with a beard in a wig and places him in the women's bathroom or women's locker room, and true to James Martin's prescription, exploits the uncertainty of that man's intentions for

---

[72] Jones, "More Say Birth Gender Should Dictate Sports Participation," para. 1.
[73] Jones, para. 10.
[74] *Coach.*

the other women in the room in hopes of activating their supporters in the fight to keep those men out.

I'd like to take a pause and ask a vital question in understanding if this issue fits my hypothesis of the culture wars. So far, we have determined that trans representation and inclusion in sports fits two out of my three theoretical denotations, to a high degree. However, the evidence I have presented, and of which I have found to be the strongest, is strictly from one side of this debate. Does this, then, mean that it can still count as a culture war? Or am I giving conservatives an unfair treatment? For one, I want to maintain that it isn't just the right using exploitative rhetoric to heighten their base's frustration with the other side in this disagreement. Very briefly looking at the Human Rights Campaign's section on trans sports you read evocative and battle-ready language designed not merely to highlight their own point, but to get supporters and allies as angry as they are. "For the last two decades, anti-LGBTQ+ politicians have attempted to sow disinformation about LGBTQ+ people's rights to score cheap political points with their base,"[75] it says on their website. This language fits my theoretical framework, sort of funnily enough, because of one word: cheap. By describing the attempt by right-wing politicians to garner support from their base as *cheap*, the HRC has inserted an intentionally negative emotional connotation with the move that is less about merely relying the underlying motivation to engage in this argument from the perspective of the politicians, but the devalue it as an inherently negative move that must be regarded as such, with

---

[75] "Get the Facts about Transgender & Non-Binary Athletes," para. 3.

anger. This isn't necessarily to say doing that is a bad or wrong thing. The HRC probably does feel the move is cheap. But by introducing this emotional language, the HRC deviates from merely relaying the material information and why it's wrong, to a heightened state of emotional frustration meant to exploit any potential ally's vulnerability and mobilize them using such language.

However, the larger question I need to answer here is this: does one side of a debate being more animated or present in the degree to which they fit within my hypothesis of the culture wars make an issue more or less of one? And with what little theoretical exploration we have done already, I think the answer is no. In order for an issue to be more or less of a culture war does not rely on if everyone involved is fulfilling the requirements my hypothesis sets up. Instead, I believe, we need to look for the degree to which the issue at its face fits the four requirements I've laid out in chapter two. In this case, the animation of one side is sufficient to theoretically entail a culture war.

Returning to the framework, does the issue of trans sports inclusion fulfill marker #3? Is there any particular identity being taken on as a part of this debate that turns activists into culture warriors that fight, to some extent, *on* this issue as a part of who they are? I found this question harder to answer than I had initially assumed it to be. The easy answer is to say yes, given the same evidence we've been relying on throughout this chapter. Nikki Haley and Vicky Hartzler *literally* ran political campaigns on the subject. However, there's a caveat to that claim. On the part of Haley, as the issue became more of a setback than an aid to her in the hopes of earning and maintaining a voter base, she dialed down the explicit rhetoric about trans issues. Hartzler lost the senate campaign she ran the "Coach" ad on featuring Lia Thomas, and hasn't always necessarily clinged to the subject for relevance. The issue with politicians as culture warriors, I've come to find, is that the nature of electoral politics complicates the theoretical establishment of a culture warrior identity. Some candidates may stay firm to their ideological positions at the risk of offending moderate voters, but many will quiet their less-than-savory social positions until they've already been elected to office. It doesn't necessarily follow, then, that they aren't culture warriors. Rather, it complicates our narrative about them insofar that it may not be the sole issue they "war" with others on. While it may maintain dominance in their personal agendas, there may also be incentive to reprioritize or re-approach the issue in a way that is more-or-less activated than they are already. Once again, variability becomes key in understanding the degree to which a culture warrior is one. And I think in this case the evidence warrants us to say yes, transgender representation and inclusion in sports has spawned plenty of part-time *and* full-time culture warriors both for and against this shift in the sports world.

And finally, unambiguous disinterest in co-partisan cooperation. Taking from my language regarding *Masterpiece Cakeshop*, I think what we'll find here is that a conceptual disinterest in co-partisan cooperation *materialized* itself in the form of a slew of anti-trans laws regarding sports in public instruction that, to this day, remain hotly contested and largely stalemated in legislative bodies across the US. In 2023, up to 23 states passed laws that directly banned transgender youth from participating in school sports aligned with their gender identity.[76] In many states, led by Republicans, these laws began at k-12 levels, but were often extended or designed to include two and four-year colleges as well, such as HB 391 and HB 261 passed by Republican Governor of Alabama Kay Ivey.[77] This has been reflected, though much less successfully, on a federal level as well with laws such as HR 734 in the House of Representatives, which was planned to enact many of the same policy shifts on transgender participation as the many state bills had.[78] Its language reflected not only the view that the participation of trans women in women's sports was really the inclusion of "biological males" but it also invalidated gender identity as a concept, claiming "sex shall be recognized based solely on a person's reproductive biology and genetics at birth." (para. 2) Taken in context of the deeply emotional rhetoric from politicians and activists, I think we can successfully determine that this issue fits the description of high disinterest in co-partisan cooperation both conceptually and materially, through the laws we're seeing litigated today.

---

[76] Gaffney, "Physicians Say Transgender Sports Bans Are a Health Issue," para. 1.
[77] Barnes, "Transgender Athletes and the Laws That Govern Participation," para. 7.
[78] Barnes, para. 2.

What Lia Thomas' story helped spark was this deeply contested question of not merely trans legitimacy in American culture, but the inclusion of transgender athletes—primarily trans *female* athletes, who are more often the target of these laws than trans male athletes[79]—in public sports. The moral panic around transgender women unfairly competing in women's titles has exploded to such a degree, you'd think this was a frequent occurrence. And while politicians may shift the degree to which they incorporate the issue into their platforms during elections, the vitriol of elected officials and their policies expresses a deep identification with a need to end the inclusion of trans people in public sports. It's also worth reviewing the stipulation we have established with this section, in that while (at least, in large part), conservatives are the more vocal side about this issue, with liberals merely reacting, that does not invalidate the theoretical framework to understanding if this is a culture war. Rather than looking for equality in partisan behavior, we're focused more on the strength of the sign in and of itself, meaning while it is Republicans who are more concerned and vocal about the issue, it is still eligible for the points on identity and rhetoric our hypothesis of the culture wars has established. If any issue was a culture war, I think this one fits the bill. However, the intricate details that distinguish the cultural aspects of it—the more existential question of trans identity and inclusion—versus the more policy-oriented issue of trans sports bans muddles our understanding. We will

---

[79] Barnes, para. 6.

return to this muddling in part three largely, when we discuss the impact of the culture wars.

Issue 3: The War on Christmas

Our third issue is often neglected by commentators insofar as it appears benign on its face. However, the substance of this debate is much richer than the layman may assume, in that it asks a very fundamental question of the United States: how secular are we going to become? Of course, I refer to the effervescent war on christmas. The fundamental issue of the war on christmas is that as America has become more and more secular, the appearance and prominence of religious paraphernalia in holiday items, celebrations and artifacts has become downplayed or outright restricted for fear of polarizing non-christian religious groups.

As far back as 1921, Henry Ford is known to have written in his antisemitic pamphlet *The International Jew* "Last Christmas most people had a hard time finding Christmas cards that indicated in any way that Christmas commemorated Someone's Birth."[80] Throughout American history, this battle has persisted. Even amidst the religious burst in the 1950s, the fear of communism took the place of the fear of pure secularism attacking the US, as journalists, politicians and world leaders bemoaned an attempt to "take Christ out of Christmas — to denude the event of its religious meaning. ... The UN fanatics launched their assault on Christmas in 1958,

---

[80] Emery, "A History of the 'War on Christmas,'" para. 6.

but too late to get very far before the holy day was at hand."[81]

How does the war on christmas fit our signifiers for the culture war? First, let's investigate the moral attitudes and the emotions they elicit. This one is difficult. When we look at data from 2017, just after former President Donald Trump was elected and "won" the war on christmas for the christian right, we might see deep emotional epitaphs from commentators at Fox News, but the Pew Research Center had found that more than half, 52% of customers didn't particularly care whether or not superstore workers greeted them with the phrase "merry christmas" or "happy holidays."[82] The question becomes this: does a disconnect between the more active elite, the "culture warriors," and the masses who may be less engaged and less concerned, mean the issue doesn't qualify for the first indicator? Theoretically, this question is difficult to answer. While the masses are not particularly animated by whether or not people say "merry christmas" the way Bill O'Reilly or Donald Trump were, there may still be an animus of frustration over the deeper issue of secular versus religious ideological authority in the US. In 2022, Pew found that a share of 45% of Americans believed the US should, in fact, be a "christian nation,"[83] though that came with the stipulation that they didn't necessarily believe religious teachings should be enshrined in law or

---

[81] Emery, para. 14.

[82] "How 'the War on Christmas' Became a Political Rallying Cry."

[83] Tevington, "45% of Americans Say U.S. Should Be a 'Christian Nation,'" para. 2.

churches should endorse candidates. Rather, they saw that christianity ought to influence the behavior of the government.[84]

Given this evidence, I'm going to say that we can qualify that the war on christmas generates a slight degree of deep morals and, to a lesser degree emotional reactions. And to further qualify this I want to investigate signifier number two: rhetorical tools and their use to extract emotional reactions and moral feelings. I think this one is stronger than the first, and is used in an attempt to further polarize people in this war on christmas. Take, for example, Bill O'Reilly's 2004 television broadcast covering the war:

Now, all of this anti-Christian stuff is absurd, and may even be a bias situation. But the real reason it's happening has little to do with Christmas and everything to do with organized religion. Secular progressives realize that America as it is now will never approve of gay marriage, partial birth abortion, euthanasia, legalized drugs, income redistribution through taxation, and many other progressive visions because of religious opposition. But if the secularists can destroy religion in the public arena, the brave new progressive world is a possibility. That's what happened in Canada.[85]

O'Reilly's statement fits our theoretical framework in its use of moralistic language in order to

---

[84] Tevington, para. 3.
[85] Emery, "A History of the 'War on Christmas,'" para. 3.

frame the issue, rather accurately, as adjacent to Christmas rather than about it particularly. Language such as "if the secularists can *destroy* religion in the public arena," and the laundry list of conservative straw men on leftist policy proposals such as gay marriage, abortion access and universal basic income. It is through this framing, O'Reilly exploits a fear of progressive ideological and policy positions and their potential impact, and the inherent bonding of them to secularism in a spiritual battle with religion, with christianity in particular, attempting to "destroy" it.

I also want to briefly look at former President Trump's rhetoric on Christmas after his election. In a tweet on Christmas eve in 2017, one year after his election to the Presidency, Trump tweeted "People are proud to be saying Merry Christmas again. I am proud to have charge against the assault of our cherished phrase. MERRY CHRISTMAS!!!!!"[86] Trump's language here also fits marker #2 by describing any attempts at deviating from the use of "merry christmas" during the holiday season as an "assault" on a "cherished phrase." Per James Martin's description of the hermeneutics of public speech, I think Trump's language does what he ascribes, and exploits an uncertainty about the future—though a much deeper fear than whether or not people will say the phrase, and rather the slippery slope fallacy of what would happen next if "they" got their way in freezing the use of the phrase—in order to extract emotions in the present to garner support.

---

[86] "How 'the War on Christmas' Became a Political Rallying Cry."

In either case, I can confidently say that the language of the war on christmas fits our hypothesis of the culture wars to a much higher degree than the deep morals or emotions. And continuing on the example of Donald Trump, I also think he's exemplar of signifier number 3: a distinct identity formed around this culture war. In a way, Trump's animation around the war on christmas during his 2016 presidential campaign and his first term in office reinvigorated this tired debate as majorities continued not to be particularly bothered. Both on the campaign trail he promised "If I become president, we're going to be saying Merry Christmas at every store,"[87] and once he was elected he declared that America had been freed. "Guess what? We're saying 'Merry Christmas' again,"[88] Trump told a crowd at the Values Voter Summit in October 2017. Since then, largely conservative voices have annually reminded the rest of us about this war and why they must defend themselves from it. Dennis Prager, a conservative radio talk show host, appeared on the *Fox & Friends* morning program in 2019 to tell their hosts that "I am deeply worried about the radical secularization of America, and the obvious arena — the most obvious, perhaps — is changing 'Christmas' into 'holiday.'"[89]

There is a new stipulation that arises when we consider this qualifier. The passion and internalization of the war on christmas is obvious on

---

[87] Hamedy, "Did Trump Stop the 'War on Christmas'? Some Say Yes | CNN Politics," para. 6.

[88] Hamedy, para. 7.

[89] Reed, "'Fox & Friends' Segment Makes Dubious Claim That 'Radicals' Are Waging a War on Christmas," para. 5.

the parts of culture warriors like Prager or Trump. But that animation is annual, not perpetual. Does the consistency with which a culture warrior maintains their identity on that specific "war" change whether or not we can even consider them a culture warrior? Not necessarily. It can be assumed to a degree that there aren't many, if any at all, "pure" culture warriors whose sole focus is one particular issue and that issue alone. Like any activists, culture warriors likely have an array of issues that they advocate for year-round, at most tied together by a common theme or ideology. However, I think we can maintain that a culture warrior is a culture warrior even if the issue only resurfaces once a year or periodically. The real focus we'd want is whether or not the period is relatively consistent. As I covered in the introduction to this section, the issue of the war on christmas has activated the emotions of culture warriors among the elite since the 1920s. In that case, I'd argue that we can say that this issue has continually animated culture warriors concerned with it consistently for over a hundred years, and maintains the qualification laid out in our third indicator of the culture wars.

Finally, does the war on christmas exude a conceptual and material disinterest in co-partisan cooperation to a degree? Similarly to the first indicator, I believe the war on christmas very loosely displays signals of disinterest in co-partisan cooperation. Commentators like Bill O'Reilly demanded boycotts against stores they deemed to be hypocritical in their cashing in on the holiday without the explicit celebration of it,[90] and while policies have

---

[90] Emery, "A History of the 'War on Christmas,'" para. 22.

been put in place to encourage more secular holiday expressions so as to capitalize on the larger secular shift in America, to express it as a disinterest in co-partisan cooperation would be grossly exaggerated, as this side doesn't even acknowledge this war, let alone care enough to refuse to cooperate with their opponents. Given that we have acknowledged one-sideism doesn't necessarily imply that the issue is not pertaining to the culture wars before, I wouldn't go so far as to claim it doesn't apply here. However, given it's very one-sided and only periodical, I'd say it's a largely conceptual disinterest that doesn't often materialize, and is very weak in general.

All in all, the war on christmas is surely a culture war. But it's not simply a war over the pure fact of whether or not Americans say "merry christmas." Instead, it's a much deeper debate on the rise in secularism and the vitriol that comes from those who see that increased secularism in public spaces as an existential threat. We've also established a new stipulation for understanding our hypothesis of the culture wars: the consistency with which a culture warrior is positioned "around" that particular issue does not have to be perpetual, and can be an annual tradition, so long as the tradition maintains over a period of time (whether that be years or months or what have you is still up to discretion and debate). We move to our final issue to apply whether our hypothesis of the culture wars holds, and will attempt to weed out any other stipulations we need to understand how to spot a culture war.

Issue 4: School Boards and the 'Parental Rights' Movement After 2020

Our final investigation remains the most active of the four we've discussed in this chapter, and as such it maintains an err of questioning around it. The idea itself of a parents responsibility to educate their children in some fashion goes back hundreds of years. More than this, the debate on how this should be done, and the Government's role in it, has been maintained. As far back as 1859, philosopher and parliamentarian John Stuart Mill wrote in his seminal work *On Liberty,* "Were the duty of enforcing universal education once admitted there would be an end to the difficulties about what the State should teach, and how it should teach, which now convert the subject into a mere battlefield for sects and parties, causing the time and labour [sic] which should have been spent in educating to be wasted in quarreling about education."[91] In the modern day, this has materialized in the US under the name of the 'parental rights movement.' This is a movement of largely conservative activists who, particularly after the Coronavirus pandemic and the contentious 2020 Presidential election, felt that the public education system by-in-large was, at the very least, unsuitable for their children. However, the more overt claim was that public education, and much of higher education as well, was a form of indoctrination that was effectively brainwashing American kids to be left-wing to some degree.

---

[91] Mill, *On Liberty,* 97.

The development and growth of public schooling in America was largely uninterrupted, suscept to the same biases as any other institution in American life of its time (segregation, sex discrimination, etc), but it was the Scopes Monkey Trial in 1925 that ignites a passion most similar to the kind of passion we see today.[92] The trial looked into a case where the state of Tennessee had banned instruction on Darwin's theory of evolution because it contradicted the religious teaching of the Bible. Other hot button issues, such as desegregation, the second red scare of the 1950s, and the sexual revolution led to a shift in the power of localities over their school boards, and the federal government through the Department of Education. Our recent battle began with COVID-19. Some parents, influenced by the heated rhetoric of political advocacy groups and culture warriors about the effectiveness and 'oppressiveness' of mask mandates, led to contentious school board meetings, a ceremony once thought to be largely litigious and droning.[93]

With that extensive context out of the way, let's apply our hypothesis of the culture wars. First, are there deep moral attitudes and the emotional reactions they elicit? I'd say there's a swath of practical evidence that supports this hypothesis. In an investigation by PBS NewsHour, Penncrest School District board member David Valesky posted on Facebook regarding LGBTQ+ friendly children's literature in their schools, saying "Besides the point of

---

[92] Lonas, "How School Boards Became One of Democracy's Front Lines," para. 17.

[93] Lonas, para. 25.

being totally evil, this is not what we need to be teaching kids. They aren't at school to be brainwashed into thinking homosexuality is ok."[94] This rhetoric is shared by other top conservative political pundits directing parents across the country to reclaim their position over members of their local school boards, especially regarding issues like Critical Race Theory, an academic and legal theory pertaining to the legacy of slavery and institutional racism and its effect on modern American institutions that conservatives have claimed are infiltrating schools through Diversity, Equity, and Inclusion efforts to indoctrinate students into believing exaggerated narratives about oppression. Charlie Kirk, political internet personality and founder of Turning Point USA, said in an interview at their AmericaFest 2023, "DEI is a marxist program that has infiltrated ... They want everyone to look different but think the same."[95]

This heated language, on many accounts at school board meetings, is reflected by parents. Across counties and localities separated by hundreds—even thousands—of miles, parents yell and berate school board members and each other and vice versa. They have become a melting pot of vitriol that, in some cases bubble up beyond their limitation, and are backed by deeply convicted moral views on the role of parents in their student's education, usually relating to these niche, even exaggerated or wholly fabricated, issues being taught and promoted on campus. Marker

---

[94] *School Boards Become Battlegrounds for Nation's Divisions on Race, Gender and More.*

[95] *"DEI Must DIE!" - Charlie Kirk Goes off Against the DEI Movement.*

number 1 is satisfied very easily and very broadly in this case in my opinion.

What of the rhetoric for this battle? Returning to Kirk's example, we see Martin's hermeneutics played out when he describes CRT, which he claims is being taught in schools, as "Marxist." He doesn't necessarily cite an example of some kind of actual Marxist ideology being taught—rather, enforced as truth—in schools on a widespread level. But by taking advantage of the uncertainty parents have about their children in public schools, given the parents aren't necessarily plugged into those school's actions, he effectively polarizes them into believing exaggerated moral claims that their children are hence being brainwashed into believing DEI initiatives in their schools are part of this nefarious plot. "What DEI does," Charlie continues, "it is retribalizing society into a new, India-style caste system, where you can never escape. No matter how much good you do, no matter how much you study, no matter how early you work, no matter how much you try to improve your life, you're trapped."[96] Kirk's claim here, beyond using a buzzword like Marixst which his followers might recognize, more directly associates DEI programs, which in large part include seminars on race relations, histories of oppression and occasionally take menial actions to acknowledge the part that systemic racism has had in a community, with more overtly oppressive policy practices. In this instance, too, he literally compares it to India's social caste system that ranks and prioritizes members of its higher order over those lower on the ladder. A parent, who already knows very

---

[96] *"DEI Must DIE!" - Charlie Kirk Goes off Against the DEI Movement.*

little of what their children are actually learning in school, will hear this and become concerned if they show up to the next school board meeting or teacher-parent conference and they hear about a DEI program being in place at the school. Kirk's manipulative hermeneutics will take hold and metastasize into further attacks by the parent themself.

Ben Shapiro, too, uses exploitative rhetoric in order to draw out the emotions of frustrated and confused parents regarding this issue. Shortly after the issue of parents rights boiled over into national discourse in about 2021, Biden Administration Attorney General Merrick Garland issued a memorandum to the President concerned with the increase in threats of physical violence being played out by lone parents, groups of parents, and in some cases coordinated threats by known terror groups like the Proud Boys. The Attorney General promised in his letter,

To this end, I am directing the Federal Bureau of Investigation, working with each United States Attorney, to convene meetings with federal, state, local, Tribal, and territorial leaders in each federal judicial district within 30 days of the issuance of this memorandum. These meetings will facilitate the discussion of strategies for addressing threats against school administrators, board members, teachers, and staff, and will open dedicated lines of communication for threat reporting, assessment, and response.[97]

Conservative activists and their followers were quick to characterize Garland's memo as a coordinated attack against these confused and concerned parents. Shapiro's comments came after a particular controversy surrounding a decision the School Board of Loudoun County, Virginia that was going to limit parent comments after much of the heated back-and-forth sessions had there, especially regarding the board's policy regarding transgender students and the elusive "Critical Race Theory" they believed was being implemented there.

In his video, Shapiro says "We've been hearing for weeks now, about these supposed domestic terrorist movements in the united states, no we're not talking about the KKK, no we're not talking about Black Lives Matter rioters, we're talking of course, about parents, who are going to school board meetings and then saying things, which is super, duper scary."[98] Shapiro's language here is seeping with an emotional exaggeration that will prime the attitudes of his audience, by characterizing Garland's comments in a way that makes it appear as if they were directed at them, who may not have attended one of these school board meetings, but now feel that

---

[97] Garland, "Office of Public Affairs | Justice Department Addresses Violent Threats Against School Officials and Teachers | United States Department of Justice."
[98] *Loudoun County School Board BLASTED Over Bombshell Daily Wire Exposé.*

while the KKK (an organization that holds no real social or political power in modern American society) and BLM 'rioters' (a historically exaggerated group of uber-violent protestors, some with ties to violent groups like Antifa, who in some isolated cases attempted to turn the largely peaceful daytime BLM protests into violent riots at night) are let off the hook, the DOJ, which is translated into the Biden Administration, which is translated into Joe Biden himself, are targeting them simply for protecting their kids and their rights. The part where people threatened to stalk, hunt down, and kill members of their school boards is conveniently left out or underplayed.

In both of the previous cases, we have evidence to say that this case fits with marker 2 in our hypothesis of the culture wars, as the rhetoric of the most active speakers for the parents rights movement speaks to the deep moral feelings these people have about particular policies in schools that protect transgender-identifying kids and teenagers, DEI programs, and mask and vaccine mandates. This taps into an uncertainty about the intentions of these school board members in an attempt to shore up antipathy against state and federal officials, through the creation of an exaggerated narrative that they are part of a more directly connected plot, led by state and local officials explicitly intending to "brainwash" the children so that they may remain in power forever. These activists and commentators exploit that uncertainty and use it to polarize their audiences and mobilize them against political opposition.

Marker 3 is more interesting, as on a national level I'd say not many of the "activists" we're seeing related to this issue are necessarily culture warriors. There have been some measures taken, however there aren't that many significant members of state or federal legislatures that have internalized this particular issue into their crux, even temporarily or annually since its explosion in around 2021. However, there was an increase in the number of groups focusing their efforts—and funds—into local school board races, trying to support and get elected some of these angry, largely conservative parents into those very boards. Millions of dollars were invested, particularly, in the 2022 midterms by groups such as the 1776 Project and Moms for Liberty,[99] but to no avail. Despite how polarizing the issue was for the parents and activists upset at school boards, that was met with a very harsh electoral rebuttal, as about half of the hundreds of candidates some of these groups endorsed had won.[100] I believe this is evidence of the internalization of the issue as an identity for these parents and groups via its use as a mobilizer. For one, to run as a member of the school board you accused of brainwashing your children is a sign that the issue matters so much you feel you must use it to solve the problem. Two, the persistence, while not particularly strong for perhaps commentators like Kirk or Shapiro who have moved onto the next thing for the large part, have stirred these local and state movements in a way that will probably have lasting effects that ought to be investigated. And while the national discourse may

---

[99] Binkley, "'Too Hyperbolic'? School Board Parental Rights Push Falters," para. 3.
[100] Binkley, para. 4.

likely return to parental rights once or twice in the future, for these parents it is a part of their everyday lives, as a show of commitment to the proper education of their children.

Lastly, and perhaps robotically I present our final marker in our final case, is conceptual and material disinterest in copartisan cooperation. We have already seen this displayed in the words and behaviors of activists, parents, commentators and organizations alike. Angry, moralistic yelling that describes what schools are teaching as "evil," groups using the threat (or promise, in some cases) of physical violence to strongarm their way in this conflict, and millions spent trying to oust current school board members in place of themselves. And even from the defense, we see strong disinterest in cooperation. Many school boards have maintained their defiance in some of their policies, including DEI or protecting trans-identifying students, or masks and closures in the face of these heated comments and threats. In one 2021 incident, members of a school board in California openly mocked parents' frustration about the schools being closed due to the concern about COVID-19 infections.[101] The ideological, that is to say, conceptual disinterest in investigating claims of indoctrination or concerns about the policies school boards were passing and their effects on student populations and families materialized into the current battle we see playing out, even to this day. While quite new, this culture war

---

[101] Colarossi, "California School Board Members Caught on Tape Mocking Parents Upset About School Closures."

shows a strong sign of disinterest in copartisan cooperation that shows very little sign of stopping.

With our case studies at hand, I have a few conclusions to draw for this chapter and Part I of this book:

Firstly, I believe we have affirmed the validity of this hypothesis of the culture wars we established in chapter two. While much more theoretical exploration will be needed to further identify the strengths and weaknesses of this hypothesis, I think these cases and the evidence presented in chapter two signify our markers/determinants of the culture wars to be a reliable indicator of a culture wars issue in a more objective sense. With this more formal hypothesis of the culture wars, we now no longer have to needlessly postulate what is or is not a culture war in endless internet debates, and can instead move into the substance of particular culture war issues and how to win them.

Second, I think we have denoted the majority of the stipulations that come with our hypothesis of the culture wars, the fact that they come in varying degrees rather than wholly, the focus on strength of culture warrior identity and not its partisan source, the limitations on how frequently a culture war must be brought up in order to maintain its status as a culture war instead of some issue your uncle brings up once every now and again. For future investigation, these stipulations will be key in order to further examine any other limitations to the hypothesis, its determinants, and their application to real-world political and social controversies.

Finally, the wider implications of Part I of this book now enable us to expand upon them in Part II. For the last 80 pages, we have been attempting to define the culture wars. I believe we have done just that. Exploring history and anthropology, we established the origins and expansion of the more fundamental essence of the culture wars, culture itself and why it comes into conflict with other cultures across time. Investigating a vast swathe of literature on psychology, hermeneutics, public policy and social attitudes and norms, we have also determined four main markers of the culture wars. And we have applied those theoretical determinants to four real-world examples that have validated their use. Now, turning to Part II, we will apply this definitional foundation to the actual "war" part of a culture war, and attempt to understand how they might actually be won, if they can be at all. I intend to do this through three particular channels.

First, we'll try to inhabit the mind of a culture warrior, and assess how they might conceptualize their strategies. Second, we will investigate the makeup of a culture wars issue, which is to say we will attempt to determine how different culture wars make use of material facts versus philosophical or moral faculties that aren't as tethered to material reality, and how that might limit the ability to "win" them. Third and finally, we will step back to ask the broader question "can the culture wars be won?" This question will be based, in part, on our conclusions in chapters four and five. It will also be twofold, asking both can *a* culture war be won and can the amalgamation of all culture wars be won? Do they combine to create one penultimate struggle for society that, eventually, can or will be bested? From these conclusions, then, we will be able to explore the impact of the culture wars on political discourse, and democratic institutions in Part III.

Part II

Winning the Culture Wars

Chapter Four

Stratagem of a Culture Warrior

In his book *The Semisovereign People* (1960) E.E. Schattschneider speaks to the very nature of conflict in politics, describing that "control of the scale of conflict has always been a prime instrument of political strategy, whatever the language of politics may have been."[102] In his assessment of political conflict, the scope or size of the conflict massively determines its outcome. In using scope, Schattschneider refers to either the *socialization* or *privatization* of conflict. By this, he refers to the ability of two actors in a conflict to get its third, unseen actor involved: the audience. By engaging the audience in the fight, or keeping it from the audience altogether, both the winners and losers of political conflict can tip the scales of power more or less in their favor.

What Schattschneider's comments on political conflict contextualize for us is the background to what will become the strategies of a culture warrior. Having established the culture wars as a hypothesis and seen them in practice, we now must attempt to get into the mind of a culture warrior as I envision them in order to understand why—and more importantly, *how*—the culture warrior engages with their opposition. Schattschneider's idea of socializing or privatizing conflict is a good place to start, as it provides us with a

---

[102] Schattschneider, "The Contagiousness of Conflict," 8.

fundamental tool if we are to win a culture war: an arsenal of fans who will decide the victor. At the very least semantically, we can "win" arguments on the culture wars through our ability to get our audience involved, as does happen every presidential election cycle. "Winners" and "losers" come and go, and their victory does not hinge upon who provides the most sound reasoning, valid arguments or elegant defense of their positions, but rather who gets the most excited audience members on their side. It is they, retrospectively, that will decide the winner of a debate based on these largely aesthetic features of it.

In my understanding of it, the culture warrior best benefits, and thus is most interested, in socializing conflict rather than privatizing it. Perhaps a byproduct of my sloppy application of Schattschneider's understanding of political conflict, but if taken with our definition of a culture warrior, we can design an idea of their motivations by understanding that, especially in the context of public debates and arguments, you'd want the inclusion of more people in order to sway the cultural milieu in your direction rather than keeping your conflict "private" in the sense that it does not spread into a more widespread debate in society.

Originally, this chapter was intended to focus on literal arguments conservative and liberal culture warriors have made. However, a much larger methodology in fighting the culture wars emerged in my investigation of talking points about them that I think is much more interesting—and useful. In general, I found that there are four broad positions culture warriors pursue in culture wars discourse. The first three are regularly pointed out, while the fourth, however, is what I demarcate as being a signal of the "extreme." In order, I call these positions: *Causal Hot Potato, Victim-Claiming, Slippery Slopsim,* and *Mutually Assured Destruction.* I want to explore these positions individually as well as a collective in order to best understand how they advance the culture wars successfully for your side, and the fallbacks that may come with using them.

Causal Hot Potato

Causal hot potato, as its name implies, is the act of throwing the blame for who "caused" the culture wars. As far as an objective reality is concerned, the origins of the culture wars as an entity is debatable, but hinges on the religious social battles happening in the late eighties and nineties we discussed briefly in our definition in Part I. "The earlier culture war really was about secularization, and positions were tied to theologies and justified on the basis of theologies," James Davison Hunter told *Politico* in 2021.[103] We saw this exemplified in Pat Buchanan's speech at the 1992 Republican National Convention, referring to the culture wars as a "religious war" in general.

However, a partisan cleavage has naturally occurred in defining when the culture wars started, and who is to blame for it. On the left, the culture wars are framed as being a few things. As Hunter noted, its focus was once largely the religious right's obsession with a pseudo-theocratic state governed by biblical laws. But many historians also contextualize it in the context of civil rights in the 1960s and the

---

[103] Stanton, "How the 'Culture War' Could Break Democracy," para. 6.

various civil liberties movements it spawned.[104] However, the framing remains that the right shifted into a more religious, almost fundamentalist state as the Republican party observed Ronald Reagan's success appealing to evangelicals. The ideological cementation of the various social movements the right opposed over time, including integration, marriage rights, abortion, and others occurred, in this inception, through the religious appeal and vitriol shored up by the GOP in its attempt to streamline and brand its opposition to these movements as a single entity that could be run on as a political platform.

On the right there is a similar conception of the culture wars from their origin. At its inception, liberals are seen as wanting relatively reasonable positions, for example, gay marriage. But, over time, conservative culture warriors contend that the left kept shifting further left with every victory, insisting that religious institutions recognize and celebrate these marriages, that children be "indoctrinated" into an LGBTQ+ "agenda" and overtly sexualized. Using our friend Ben Shapiro as an example, he says in a video on the origin of the culture wars,

The rush to the left on social issues from the left is unbelievable. Remember, Bill Clinton in the 1990s, being a pro-abortion politician, still said things like 'safe, legal, and rare.' There was a baseline acknowledgement that abortion was a bad thing. Now, the left speaks out about how wonderful abortion is, abortion is an asset. Don't tell me that the

---

[104] Alfonseca, "Culture Wars," para. 5.

right has gotten more right wing, that's just a lie. All that happened is that the right stopped surrendering on every single issue.[105]

Shapiro's characterization, which follows to further claim the left intentionally polarizes the nation on once "uncontroversial" supposed facts, encapsulates the conservative position in the game of causal hot potato. And if you have been paying attention, you'll notice both sides underpin a similar theme: that one side has remained the same, grounded in the same values that side has always been grounded in, while the other has become extremist and started the culture wars as a political tool. This is the core of causal hot potato, and is seen echoed throughout culture wars discourse. In a 2021 blog, columnist Kevin Drum writes "It is not conservatives who have turned American politics into a culture war battle. It is liberals. And this shouldn't come as a surprise: Almost by definition, liberals are the ones pushing for change while conservatives are merely responding to whatever liberals do."[106]

Casual hot potato has a key function for culture warriors that makes it indispensable, and thus a mainstay, of culture wars discourse. Through the reframing of the origins of the culture wars, culture warriors too can reframe the discursive value of the discourse of the culture wars. By reframing the culture wars as being the *fault* of or being *started* by the other side, a culture warrior opens the possibility to then

---

[105] *BOOM: Shapiro SETTLES Culture War ORIGINS Debate.*
[106] Drum, "If You Hate the Culture Wars, Blame Liberals," para. 3.

make broader, moral statements about the other side that can discredit their defense. The culture wars do not have a particularly positive reputation, as such being the one who instigated them makes you the villain. By assigning and reassigning that label in debate, both the left and the right intend to reframe the discourse further to assign that negative value to the other side inherently, essentially asking the rhetorical question to the audience "what kind of person would start the culture wars?" with the tacit answer they're fishing for being *a bad person.*

In successfully reframing the origins of the culture wars, which remains a sort of on-going struggle, a culture warrior gives themself the power to further discursively reconstruct the value of the argument, its intentions, the inherent villains and heroes, and the moral imperative the audience has in joining in on their side to defeat the villain. I borrow language such as "heroes" or "villains" from Dr Elizabeth Anker's exploration of the conventions of melodrama as a political discourse, where she finds "melodramatic political discourse designates political actors and agency through characters of victims, villains, and heroes."[107] She contends that these labels coincide with the first convention which she calls its moral economy. The moral economy of melodramatic political discourse, Anker writes, "shapes its depictions of political events and national identity. Good equates to the U.S. nation-state, evil equates to the sources of national injury, and as these moralized identities circulate they reinforce each other—so that

---

[107] Anker, *Orgies of Feeling,* 33.

claims of national goodness are enabled and sustained by the injuries caused by evil Others."[108]

I believe we can apply these conventions of melodramatic political discourse to our hypothesis of the culture wars as part of the strategic decisions culture warriors make in framing and engaging in the battles that constitute them. Much how Anker's description of a moral economy in which good and evil, broadly and presumably purely defined, distinctifies national identities, so too have we determined a moral economy defines the culture wars (Marker one: deep moral attitudes and the emotional reactions they elicit). Furthermore the incorporation of these deep moral inceptions of the culture wars into the identities of culture warriors fits Anker's description of melodramatic political discourse. From a strategic position, then, the reframing of the culture wars' origin allows for broader reconstruction that, in the same vein as Anker's description, reinforces the moral attitudes of a culture warrior as well as the moral economy of the culture war at hand. As we have previously discussed, the reconstruction of the culture wars as being propagated by the other side allows us to moralize their identity and affiliation with it as bad, thus reinforcing our own inherent goodness.

Victim-Claiming

One of the byproducts of a culture warrior's reconstruction of the culture wars as being their opponent's fault is to then also claim that those culture wars were started by the other side with the explicit intention to target them. *The culture wars are*

---

[108] Anker, 32.

their fault, and they're instigating them against me. As its name and this description insinuates, a culture warrior will attempt to reframe themselves in the context of the culture wars as being the victim, thus lending more leverage to themselves as someone worth getting involved in the battle for from the perspective of the audience. Similar to Schattschnieder's inception of it, it would be the "loser" who calls for reinforcements in the hopes that it would bolster them to a fighting chance.[109] If we replace his language of winners and losers with a more moralized language of victims and aggressors to fit the moral economy from Dr Anker's melodramatic political discourse, we can see a similar effect. A *victim* would call in more attention to the conflict in order to bolster support for them in the hopes it will keep them from dying. An *aggressor* would privatize the conflict so as to kill the victim and effectively succeed in their mission to "win" that culture war.

Returning to Ben Shaprio's characterization of the culture wars, his framing allows for a conservative victimization to be undergone that pits the left as being an aggressor in the culture wars. In this reframing, the right then can claim to be a victim of the culture wars as opposed to a warrior in them, in hopes to bring in more people to the right as support. In a letter to conservative members of the house, Representative Jim Banks (R-IN) said "We are in a culture war. On one side, Republicans are working to renew American patriotism and rebuild our country. On the other, Democrats have embraced and given a platform to a radical element who want to tear

---

[109] Schattschneider, "The Contagiousness of Conflict," 16.

America down."[110] Banks' framing of the culture wars further victimizes the right as being on a defensive against an aggressive and evil left, which is characterized using strong emotive language and blankly accused of intending to "tear America down." Returning to Anker's conventions of melodramatic political discourse, she says "In [Frederich] Nitetzche's concept of the venomous eye, evil is not just the constitutive opposite of goodness; it actively aims to harm goodness." (p. 32) This tracks with the examples we have explored, and contextualizes them as a strategy. It is through the reconstruction of the culture wars as a crusade that we, as the culture warrior, are a victim of that allows for us to call for help from the audience who may not be involved, and become personally engaged in the subject. If the other side doesn't just attack us, but attack us as innocent victims, they become the villains we spoke of earlier, justifying the audience not just helping us to safety, but joining us in opposing that other side given their villainous reconstruction.

It is through this reconstruction, too, that our victimization legitimizes another practice in the culture wars also observed by Anker's conventions of melodramatic discourse. "Melodramatic political discourse," she writes, "emphasizes the experience of powerlessness in order to chart a course of action that will restore the power of the virtuous."[111] The act of victimization, in Anker's description of it, is not merely the assertion of victimhood. It is the

---

[110] Banks, "Lean Into Culture War | Republican Study Committee," para. 4.
[111] Anker, *Orgies of Feeling*, 36.

experience of overwhelming powerlessness at the hands of the evil Other, due to circumstances out of the control of the victim. In victim-claiming, this is observed through the lens of "the (left/right) moving to the extreme (left/right)" claims made by culture warriors. This shift is contextualized as a hostile takeover, that through allowing the permission of liberal or conservative beliefs in discourse, and further allowing liberal or conservative bills to pass in congress, we as the victims are now subject to a society that has been vaguely overtaken by the other side and intends to oppress or destroy us. Furthermore, in line with Anker's writing, this experience of overwhelming powerlessness that constitutes our abject victimhood legitimizes the use of forceful retaliation. This is the "course of action" that the experience of victimhood will create for us that Anker writes of.

In Nietzsche's analysis, the venomous eye is a critical strategy of power born of fear, rage, and impotence, a way to condemn conditions of unfreedom, to mark them as unfair and unjust. But the identity of goodness it produces also legitimates and even enables retribution as a way to gain power over what it experiences as dominating. (p. 36)

This is the true goal of victim-claiming. Beyond merely amassing support for the victim, a culture warrior wants to legitimize the use of violence against the aggressor in the near future by highlighting the nature of their relationship with us as their victim. We are not merely attempting to appeal to the audience as a helpless overwhelmed victim who needs support to live, but we want to stir the same deep emotions we have towards our constructed aggressor in that audience as our prospective allies. Should we be successful, we can effectively socialize the conflict in our favor and, as Anker puts it, gain power over the experience of domination through the destruction of the aggressor who perpetrates it against us. More to come in a few pages.

Slippery Slopism

There are certain contexts in which the reconstruction of the culture wars as an offense started by our political opponents against us as helpless victims falls flat with audiences. Worse, we may be caught in a double-bind where practically we need the support of the other side in the legislature, thus needing to promote bipartisanship, while simultaneously wishing to retain partisan control of our audiences in the culture wars, thus needing to promote the other side's villainy. Culture warriors employ what I have so cleverly decided to dub "slippery slopism" in contexts such as these in order to play both sides without losing any major political capital.

The essence of slippery slopism is simple: While perhaps a useful ally temporarily, the other side cannot be fully trusted or supported given the potentiality for their (or their position's) evil to be realized. The slippery slope presented is that by empowering them we may find unintended consequences including the development of extremist and oppressive political actors in the long run. The slippery slope may also be presented in the context of elections, that support for a candidate or their party does not seem like an inherently dangerous thing to do, but the possibility of empowering them to embolden their extremities is a risk that isn't worth taking, and we'd be better off if you stayed with the safe, good side (us).

The slippery slope behaves, as well, as a form of moral insurance against detractors and those who question the culture warrior's intentions or claims. By way of the slippery slope, the culture warrior can assume two things: First, that they have warned the audience of the other side's potential evil, thus giving them a license to hypocritically ally with them temporarily on the basis that they did so only to achieve some short-term goal that required their opposition's support. This also recuses the culture warrior from claims of vagueness or retrospective moralization of the audience's support for the other side. Detractors can't claim that the culture warrior did *not* warn them of the other side's potential for evil or failed to do so clearly and then, once the audience has already allied with them, attack them for aligning with the other side's villainy. Second, the slippery slope allows the culture warrior to draw a firm line in the sand for the audience. If the potential for evil has been established, or furthermore if that potentiality is said to increase by way of joining the other side, the culture warrior can justify assaulting the audience if they defy the warning and join the other side anyway.

Slippery slopism is totalitarian in nature. It behaves to prevent the audience from joining the other side of a culture war by setting a firm moral boundary that cannot be crossed by the audience. To cross it in defiance of the culture warrior's sage warning against it is an act of treason that rarely can be rectified. This behavioral trait on the part of the culture warrior can be destructive, and dissolve necessary allyships, but is seen as important to the culture warrior. Remember, a real culture warrior does not just dedicate themselves to the movement for fun or for money. To them, even if only to a particular degree, the issue (the culture war, the conflict, etc) is truly a matter of good and evil. Thus, setting the boundary for the audience is supposed to be proof of that clear moral cleavage between either side, and demand allegiance to the obvious hero and clear victim in the conflict.

However, as briefly stated before, slippery slopism is also hypocritical in nature. The reality of divided party government is that in order to get things done you must strike a compromise with the other side to pass bills, or win a supermajority and ignore their cries of being steamrolled altogether. But for the audience, this can appear hypocritical as well, and may have political ramifications outside the culture warrior's control. The fundamental issue with slippery slopism in practice is that after spending so much time writing off their opposition as an evil villain, to align with or cooperate with that evil villain appears as either a corruption of the culture warrior's character, which they had spent all this time defining as the antithetical good to the villain's evil. Worse, it may come across as what it actually is, completely hypocritical. By cooperating with the other side, even if its on a non-related issue to the culture war they've been lambasted for, the culture warrior may harm their credibility and reveal that the culture war itself musn't be as world-ending as they promote it as being if they're willing to cross the aisle for other political issues.

During the House scramble for a speaker after the impeachment of Kevin McCarthy (R-CA), while majorities wanted the new speaker to cross the aisle and work with Democrats, 59% of Republicans polled wanted the new speaker to be loyal to Donald Trump, while 84% of self-reported "MAGA" Republicans wanting loyalty.[112] If the new Speaker had defied this, republicans who had been told to work with Democrats would enable their radical leftist agenda may either assume that's what the new speaker was doing, or that the Democrats weren't as radical as the culture warriors in the GOP had claimed, in either case hurting the GOP's political capital. This claim would need further investigation to confirm, but I think it holds a theoretical reality that can be observed practically.

Finally, slippery slopism relates to our undercurrent of a culture warrior's goal to reconstruct the culture wars by employing the warning of extremism as the pretext for victimization. If support for the other side contributes to their realization of evil, then the supposed instigation of and victimization that occurs as a result of the culture wars is, in part or in whole, the result of the slippery

---

[112] Salvanto, Pinto, and Backus, "Should the next House Speaker Work across the Aisle?," fig. 3.

slope. Just as it acts as a moral insurance to justify attacking the audience for picking the "wrong" side, it also acts as a precursor for the self-victimization of the culture warrior for other potential audiences as proof of that victimhood and aggression on the part of the other side.

Mutually Assured Destruction

I said that the fourth strategy of the culture warrior was, unlike the first three, a sign of extremism. As we have touched on already, a culture warrior's final strategy, why they employ these tactics to begin with, has to do with the discursive reconstruction of the culture wars as being the fault of their opponent, as being an attack that they are the overwhelmed victim of, and as being the result of enabling a slippery slope that previous audiences have engaged with by joining the other side. However, once all other options have been gone through, a culture warrior is presented with two primary options.

First, as I believe most culture warriors do, they can recycle the first three strategies for different prospective audiences. In this way, the culture warrior continues to socialize the conflict and very simply it either appeals to an audience and gains their side more supporters or fails and either gives the other side those supporters or alienates the audience altogether, benefiting nobody. Second, and more rarely, can a culture warrior continue down the path of aggression towards the audience upon the pretexts they have laid out through their victim-claiming and slippery slope claims. I quoted Elizabeth Anker in saying "the identity of goodness [Nietzche's

'Venomous Eye'] produces also legitimates and even enables retribution as a way to gain power over what it experiences as dominating."[113] She expands this comment in her final convention of political melodrama: that its conclusion is the triumph of freedom. (p. 36) In this instance, the triumph of freedom means a kind of freedom that is totally unconstrained from the overwhelming oppression by the aggression of the evil other, which is what necessitates their destruction. Applying political melodrama to the culture wars, I believe this lays the groundwork for what I call Mutually Assured Destruction.

"Mutually Assured Destruction" (or MAD) is borrowed from the era of nuclear proliferation between the United States and Russia during the cold war. In principle, it believed that at a point both superpowers contained enough nuclear armaments that, if launched by one, would trigger an equal (if not disproportionate) response by the other, destroying both nations and everyone else as a result.[114] Applying the nuclear fears of the cold war as a metaphor for the culture wars, I believe a similar principle occurs discursively. As we have already explored, the culture warrior may employ the strategies we have discussed with the broad intention to stake deep moral claims about the issue at hand for the audience, victimizing themselves as caught in the aggression of the other side, and begging for their audience to take part on their side to help fend off this evil other. However, as

---

[113] Anker, *Orgies of Feeling*, 36.

[114] "Danger of Mutually Assured Destruction - Managing the Cold War 1962-85 - Higher History Revision," para. 3.

we have also already stated, the goal is not merely to defend from the other side, but to destroy them as the source of the victim's (the culture warrior's) suffering.

The assumption of MAD in the culture wars is that both sides of a culture war are culture warriors, or led by culture warriors, and that both sides are engaging in MAD at the same time. This assumption may not necessarily hold if two sides are engaging at different levels of aggression at a certain point in their conflict. The assumption that both sides are (or are led by) culture warriors is going to be applied as a given due to our success in chapter three at applying our hypothesis of the culture wars practically. However, could we find a conflict in which one side has escalated tensions to the point of mutually assured destruction while the other side is still merely engaged in causal hot potato or victim-claiming? I believe that the nature of mutually assured destruction implies that both sides will be engaged with it simultaneously, not independently of one another but as a result of the escalation of the conflict.

Mutually assured destruction in the culture wars begets mutually assured destruction from the other side by nature of its escalatory engagement. Through the deployment of MAD by one side, the other is forced into a position where they can further escalate their own discourse to a proportionately aggressive stance. For instance, if one side of a conflict has escalated to a position of mutually assured destruction, a culture warrior has a license to say that side: started a culture war as evidenced by their intense passion against our side; is waging the culture war against our side as evidenced by their aggression against us; and was bound to behave this way as a result of the slippery slope presented in supporting or enabling their behavior. The act of mutually assured destruction permits and possibly intends for a culture warrior to escalate their own discourse so as to further villainize and legitimate opposition to them.

Mutually assured destruction addresses the concern of de-escalation by making it an unfavorable response to its aggression. A concern of culture warriors who employ MAD as a tactic to instill aggression from opponents may be that the other side won't escalate their behavior and discourse to an equally frustrated level. The goal of MAD is not merely to become so enraged at the other side that you place their destruction as a necessity for your victory in the culture war, but that it brings out their own aggression as a response which can then be used as evidence of the other side's evil and justifies your aggression against them as a form of self defense that was proactively engaged. The concern of de-escalation is avoided in the use of MAD by the antagonization of the other side's refusal to become aggressive as an admission of defeat. If the other side doesn't escalate, the culture warrior can tout that refusal as a sign of either the weakness of their position or character, effectively achieving what Anker described as gaining power over the dominating force that is our opponent. We can accomplish the status of hero from our victimhood by "defeating" the other side as evidenced by their de-escalation tactics. This puts culture warriors in a bind to either become the perceptive—or literal—loser of the conflict at hand or become more aggressive, further frustrating the conflict as a whole.

The nature of mutually assured destruction makes it so that to remain effective in a culture war one must become aggressive and confrontational, further steeped in the conflict and thus tethered to it.

Mutually assured destruction materializes both discursively and literally in instances of physical violence, giving it a reputation of extremism. So far, we have discussed MAD as a largely symbolic element of culture war strategy. Engaging in violent, confrontational discourse is one thing, but to become physically confrontational or violent is another, and I believe it can and does materialize in certain instances birthed as a result of MAD. Particularly, I believe the physical manifestation of MAD can be recognized in instances of protest, isolated instances of violence, or the development of political and systemic actions by governments and organizations to harm or suppress groups. The evolution from discourse to action can be difficult to track, and may not be the result of a single instance of rhetoric inspiring violent behavior. But a series of events can lead to the endorsement of and use of violent behavior in politics.

One 2023 study found that uncertainty about the stability and value of American democracy may have played a part in openness to political violence. They say "Most Americans across the political spectrum now perceive a serious threat to democracy in the USA,"[115] and that through this perception of a threat to democracy or of democracy's failure in certain regards, violence was a suitable answer to save

---

[115] Wintemute et al., "Views of Democracy and Society and Support for Political Violence in the USA," 2.

the country. While constituting a minority of their respondents, and limited in nature, we can glean from these findings that the employment of the rhetoric of MAD in discourse, rhetoric which often frames democracy as being under an existential threat as a result of one side or party, we prime our followers to believe in the legitimate use of violence to "save" the country from this exaggerated threat.

Stratagem of a Culture Warrior

A culture warrior may employ the use of many case-specific tactics in order to perceptively or literally win a culture war. However, there are four primary strategies that encompass the larger stratagem that the culture warrior is likely to engage in to maintain relevancy and engage broader audiences in their conflicts with ideological opponents. These tactics include; *causal hot potato*, to reframe the culture wars as the fault of the other side; *victim-claiming*, to reconstruct oneself as the victim of the culture wars instigated by the other side as the aggressor; *slippery slopism*, to construct the villain's aggression as a result of enabling by previous audiences unaware of their potential for evil; and in certain cases *mutually assured destruction*, to argue that the villain has become such an existential threat that the only solution is their complete destruction, discursively and perhaps physically.

There may well be limitations to the application of these strategies, but I believe they provide us with the most comprehensive overview of the logic of the culture warrior when engaged in conflict with their opponents, and how they may employ certain tactics in order to engage and polarize their audiences as members of the conflict rather than passive observers of it. I want to conclude by drawing out this underlying current of the strategies of the culture wars, as well. The engagement and eventual adoption of audiences as prospective allies in the culture wars is the primary strategy that supersedes all others for the culture warrior. Through the reconstruction of the culture wars broadly, the culture warrior aims to make further warriors from their audience. The further nonpartisanship of an audience serves no purpose to the culture warrior, and the act of "winning" the culture wars requires an overwhelming support of an active and engaged audience. I used the example of audiences at political debates between candidates at the beginning of this chapter, and I think it is this example that encapsulates the essence of the stratagem of the culture warrior. The act of winning a culture war, based on this stratagem, should also not cling to the production of new knowledge or most eloquent defense of material facts, but the ability of the culture warrior to employ tactics such as the ones we've discussed to excite the most audience members over the aesthetic qualities of the debate itself. Through this aesthetic colorization, I believe the culture warrior finds true victory in discourse, which can then be translated into public policy at a later point.

Chapter Five
Culture Wars Aestheticism

In order to best understand how we might win the culture wars, I believe we must turn now to the aesthetics of the culture wars in order to understand their ability to reshape our understanding of them subjectively so that we may perceive their victories and losses acutely. We have discovered culture war aesthetics in tandem with the stratagem of the culture warrior, by no accident. Aesthetics and the means through which a culture warrior will declare victory in their discursive battle with opponents are inherently tied in culture wars discourse. And it is through this exploration of the system of aesthetics that constructs the culture wars broadly in relation to their material factors that we will further understand what "winning" the culture wars may look—or more accurately, feel like.

Of course, I do not assume aesthetics comes first hand to most casual readers, and hope to discuss them descriptively and their relationship to politics broadly so that we can discuss their association with the culture wars. Aesthetics are an ambiguous branch in philosophy that, often by intention due to their vague definitions, are employed to confuse discourse. However, there are certain aspects of aesthetics that are highly relevant to politics and, particularly in our case the culture wars that I intend to argue makeup aesthetics for our uses. For one broad view of it, aesthetics is generally concerned in an artistic context: think of the value of art as an example. Art, generally, is valued on a distinct feeling that, as Martin Jay (1992) puts it is "often, but not always, identified with something known as beauty." (p. 43) This value of "beauty" can be thought of as a kind of shorthand for aesthetic value in a sense. Aesthetics approaches a subject from a position that one may be assumed to approach art. In search for the distinct feeling of "beauty" relies on determinations of color, form, shape, and design. This feeling of "beauty," I believe in a social or political sense, can be also linked to the feeling of "goodness," which we have also discussed ad nauseum thus far. The feeling of "goodness" is part of, bound to, or the same as the feeling of "beauty" in the aesthetic sense. All things associated with goodness that we have discussed, including ideas of righteousness and moral clarity are part of this aesthetic construction of politics.

Jacques Rancière (2009) puts it that, "What aesthetics refers to is not the sensible. Rather, it is a certain modality, a certain distribution of the sensible." (p. 1) This definition will, too, help us understand aesthetics in the culture wars by giving us a license to divide the "sensible," which I believe to be in reference to what we might call that which we can "sense" into two distinct categories. Using Kant's *Critique of Judgement* as a guiding text, Rancière continues that Kant distinguishes these multiple "senses" by what he calls "faculties," "between a faculty that offers the given and a faculty that makes something out of it." (p. 1) Using Kant's example of a palace, he clarifies these faculties as being the faculty of knowledge and the faculty of sensation. The faculty of knowledge, Rancière says, "defines a certain view of the palace; the palace is seen as the achievement of an idea imposed on space and on raw materials, as in a plan drafted by an architect."[116] This faculty, for our purposes, can be narrowly redefined as being concerned with *material* reality. It approaches an object from a position which is concerned largely with the material information needed to engage the object. As explained in Kant's example of a palace, the faculty of knowledge is concerned with the material reality of the plan drafted by an architect which took advantage of space and raw materials to make the physical object of the palace.

Somewhat conversely, Rancière continues that the second sense we can distinguish "views the palace as an object of pride, jealousy, or disdain."(p. 2) This faculty, which Rancière calls the "law of desire," can be narrowly redefined as *immaterial* reality. This reality approaches the object from a position that is concerned with the aforementioned value of "beauty" or "goodness." It is a sort of moral-emotional value placed on the object that gives it extra-material meaning that can itself be discerned separate from and imposed upon the material object as its symbolic physical equivalent. Using Kant's example of the palace, where the object of the palace may be void of this moral-emotional value of "beauty," we may interpret one from it that is consequently imposed onto the object of the palace that, in this view the sense of the palace supersedes the objective view of the palace as a form of knowledge. Rancière also

---

[116] Rancière, "The Aesthetic Dimension," 2.

distinguishes a third sense, which rather than hierarchically ordering one sense over the other, negates the either/or of the object.

"The aestheticization of politics in these cases," Martin Jay (1992) says, "repels … because of the chilling way in which nonaesthetic criteria are deliberately and provocatively excluded from consideration [of nonaesthetic objects, such as the 1893 French Chamber of Deputies bombing]."[117] This aestheticization of politics Jay refers to is in reference to a rise in political fascism, which we will explore later in part III, but it also alludes to themes important to understand the aestheticism of the culture wars. Aestheticism's disregard for nonaesthetic criteria of an object is a central part of culture wars aestheticism that allows for much of the discursive reconstruction of an issue we discussed in chapter four. It may not be that culture war aestheticism completely disregards the *material* reality we established earlier, but that through the division of material and immaterial reality, culture war aestheticism may then place them in a hierarchy as espoused by Rancière (2009). Through the establishment of a hierarchical relationship between the "senses," between material and immaterial reality, culture wars aestheticism establishes a heightened importance in the immaterial *over* the material that can then be discursively exploited by the culture warrior.

---

[117] Jay, "'The Aesthetic Ideology' as Ideology; Or, What Does It Mean to Aestheticize Politics?," 44.

Culture wars aestheticism aims to give the impression of immaterial reality as being, or being of the same value as, material facts. Continuing off of what we have just established, the aesthetics of the culture wars places immaterial and material reality in a hierarchy that immaterial reality takes precedence in. However, the interpretive and constructive nature of immaterial reality as a sense does not negate the need to present it in the same class as its material counterparts. Where Rancière (2009) establishes that the third way approaches sensibles in aesthetics negates the either/or of desire and knowledge, making them equals, culture wars aesthetics aim to give the impression of this third way while simultaneously placing the brunt of the discursive value in immaterial reality as being congruent with reality itself while material reality becomes reduced to being a mere technicality. Jay (1992) describes it thusly,

In the case of the "aesthetic ideology" criticized by [Paul] de Man, Eagleton and other contemporary literary critics ... The aesthetic in question is not understood as the opposite of reason, but rather as its completion, not as the expression of an irrational will, but as the sensual version of a higher, more comprehensive notion of rationality, not as the wordless spectacle of images, but as the realization of a literary absolute.[118]

---

[118] Jay, 46.

Culture wars aesthetics establish an absolute truth value to base its interpretive abilities around. The expression of aesthetics as a completion of reason, an expression of higher rationality, is one channel through which proponents of "aesthetic ideology" at one time, and culture wars aesthetics today canonize immaterial reality and its interpretative power not as an exaggeration of material reality, but its complementary. In the case espoused by Jay (1992), it is the completion of a literary absolute. But in the case of the culture wars, I believe you will find, the goal has a similar effect to the end of establishing a single unit of "truth" that all things combine to create. An aesthetic of an uncomplicated, absolute value of truth that commands reality—immaterial and material—is an invaluable discursive tool from which culture warriors rely on to assert the values of "goodness" and "beauty." The aesthetics of the culture wars are incompatible with ideas of a complex and ambiguous series of "truths" that are materially diverse and interpretively subjective. Especially in the context of "winning" the culture wars, to accept this idea of reality being a series of true things that contain little moral-emotional value that can be universally enforced is suicide. Through the assertion of immaterial reality as material reality's completion, the culture warrior can assert an idea of absolute "truth" that commands a whole, complete reality that can then be discursively argued for or against as a single unit. This unification of truth as a single object, alongside the heightened importance of immaterial reality in the hierarchy of desire and knowledge, creates the conditions in which assertions of "goodness" can be made against opponents whose opposition to said "goodness" can be redefined as antithetical to both this single unit of "truth" and the value of "goodness" that has been constructed.

Culture wars aestheticism designs unambiguous and unchanging moral typologies that are realized through experiences. Jay (1992) writes that "de Man claims that 'the aesthetic is, by definition, a seductive notion that appeals to the pleasure principle, a eudamonic [sic] judgment that can displace and conceal values of truth and falsehood likely to be more resilient to desire than values of pleasure and pain.'"[119] The construction of "goodness" comes not merely as its own object, but as we have previously discovered alongside—in fact, literally in the place of or parallel to truth itself. This is the first part of moral construction. Good and bad are not merely values that can be ascribed to amoral objects, such as in Kant's example of the palace which can be separated into two senses. Rather, the process of separating material and immaterial reality serves the purpose of re-merging them as one single object that is analogous to truth itself. What is true is also good, and what is good must be true. This revelation of true goodness comes through what Paul de Man finds to be tethered to desire than mere pleasure and pain. Jay continues, "an aestheticized politics would thus be seductively promising sensual pleasures, such as oneness with an alienated nature, it could never deliver." (p. 48) Jay (1992) denotes two important features of aestheticized politics that, in his work he claims marxist proponents of its value may not be so

---

[119] Jay, 48.

ready to accept. One, he affirms what he will later explicitly call the "rich if confusing realm of particular experience." (p. 49) These revelations of true goodness are affirmed not by the laborious ethics and logical establishments of a segregated immaterial and material reality. Rather, their remarriage through the phenomenon of experience affirms the prioritization of immaterial reality hierarchically over material reality while, as we have established previously, reuniting the two as one and as being a completion of "the truth." Two, Jay criticizes aesthetic politics for its promises of the sensual pleasures that will construct our reality of true goodness when it can't actually provide those pleasures materially. Aesthetic politics resides within a realm of immaterial reality, a reality of interpretation and emotion. Feelings of oneness with an alienated nature, or feelings of righteousness once vanquishing an enemy in a culture war, can't actually be provided by aesthetic politics. Yet, aesthetic politics uses the prospect of those feelings to engage its audiences how it needs them to be engaged.

Culture wars aesthetics constructs the experiences it intends its audiences to have as a predicate for soliciting certain emotions that align with its moral typology. The basis of this view lies chiefly with the assumption of the "aesthetic experience," which Alan Goldman paraphrases Dewey in highlighting "the indissoluble connection between cognition and the other mental faculties, mainly perception and emotion, in aesthetic experience."[120] This reaffirms what we discovered previously, where the merging of the immaterial (namely, in this case

---

[120] Goldman, "The Broad View of Aesthetic Experience," 328.

the emotional experience of aesthetics) and the material realities of our universe creates a single experience that individuals perceive unilaterally. Rancière further solidifies this view in detailing two criticisms of the assertion of the disinterested aesthetic judgment, one which claims to separate the sensibles of knowledge and desire, material and immaterial reality. The disinterested judgment claims to effectively give a "pure" observation of the aesthetic object free of the either/or, and the classes that arise from their perceptions. Rancière distinguishes the sociological criticism as finding that the notion of the disinterested judgment is an illusion.

The disinterested aesthetic judgment is the privilege of only those who can abstract themselves— or who believe that they can abstract themselves—from the sociological law that accords to each class of society the judgments of taste corresponding to their ethos, that is, to the manner of being and of feeling that their condition imposes upon them. Disinterested judgment of the formal beauty of the palace is in fact reserved for those who are neither the owners of the palace nor its builders. It is the judgment of the petit-bourgeois intellectual who, free from the worries of work or capital, indulges him- or herself by adopting the position of universal thought and disinterested taste.[121]

---

[121] Rancière, "The Aesthetic Dimension," 7.

It is this distinction that culture wars aesthetics cling to in order to establish its moral typology, the framework in which it will design experiences that then reinforce it for prospective audiences. Through the remerging of immaterial and material reality and the tacit emphasis on immaterial aesthetic experience as analogous to "the truth," culture wars aesthetics designs a single, all encompassing truth value it can argue for the existence and importance of. Subsequently, the negation of disinterested judgment and the "third way" described by Rancière (2009) forces audiences to accept culture wars aesthetic's "truth" as non-negotiable. Through mediums of light, color, sound, perspective and other artistic tools, different mediums of communication can then aesthetically frame issues into the moral typology it has constructed, and set up what may be effectively described as insurance for defiance from this superior morality.

I want to clarify my own vagueness on what the "moral typology" that culture wars aesthetics constructs actually is. The reason I have yet to define this typology is in large part because I refer not to a single moral construction that all culture wars aestheticism produces, but the broader idea of moral construction that our political actors, namely culture warriors themselves construct. I want to refer back to chapter four here as our reference point. The moral typology of the culture wars is truly the moral typology established by a culture warrior along their preferred ideological belief system. This typology is then established, as we have already discussed, by means of the stratagem of the culture warrior, the various discursive tools through which political actors will apply and move the value of political content and how audiences respond to it.

In Goldman's (2013) work, which is a criticism of Peter Kivy and Noël Carroll's narrow view of the phenomenon of the aesthetic experience, he finds that the narrow view wrongfully excludes perception of form as being part of the aesthetic (and in this case, the artistic) experience. Goldman writes, "Thus, in [Carroll's] passage, although perception of form is the paradigm for aesthetic experience, the engagement of one's recognitional capacity as recognition of content is excluded." [122] In Goldman's broader view, form is just as much a part of the aesthetic experience as it is the framework for which aesthetic experience occurs. He later uses the example of a novel to demonstrate this point, asserting that "experiencing how the characters develop and events ensue in a fictional narrative, and how those sequences are presented in the order of the narrative, *is* experiencing the structure of the novel[.]"[123] In a literal interpretation of Goldman's claim, the use of form, or rather the experience of form, sets a basis for the broader aesthetic experience about to come. While some like Kivy and Carroll may find that this experience of form ought to be separated from the aesthetic experience, I think Goldman's interpretation is far more reliable in our case than is theirs. Culture wars aesthetics, as well, are bound to no set uses of form either. This free creative license to employ any use of form imaginable to convey the culture warriors intended messaging

---

[122] Goldman, "The Broad View of Aesthetic Experience," 323.
[123] Goldman, 328.

creates the conditions under which many of the strategies and behaviors in culture wars discourse can occur. But it is the emotive attitudes that culture wars aesthetics attempts to construct that is the goal of its use of form, as Goldman finds.

Goldman (2013) criticizes both Carroll and Kivy for the exclusion of cognition in the aesthetic experience. He cites Carroll's inclusion of cognition as an organizing force external to the aesthetic experience, categorizing works in ways that he calls "relevant to appreciating their structure." (p. 326) Much like the appreciation of form, Carroll is cited as seeing the cognition of works as separate to the aesthetic experience, an external force that facilitates it but is not part of it. Likewise to his first criticism, Goldman finds that "For [Monroe C.] Beardsley as well as [John] Dewey, appreciation of aesthetic value is not limited to the perception of aesthetic properties usually cited as such, but consists in the full and harmonious engagement of different mental capacities, prominently including both perception and emotional response."[124] Using Monroe Beardsley and John Dewey as his counter-support, Goldman argues that in order to experience what may be considered the "full" aesthetic experience, one must include perception and cognition, in both an intellectual and emotional respect. The appreciation of works, in Goldman's broader view, is not consistent of Carroll's narrow understanding of the appreciation of a work's achievement of its intended purpose, which deflects all other mental and emotional capacities as being

---

[124] Goldman, 326.

defects that block such an appreciation.[125] Goldman supports this counter to Carroll and Kivy's narrow view in reference to the idea of the aesthetic experience removing us from our world. He claims that the removal from "our world" into the world of the work vis a vis the aesthetic experience was not proof of being distanced from work but being wholly absorbed by them, engaged in every detail to such a degree that we become consumed by the alternate existence of the work itself.[126] He finds that "In any case, the broader theory that includes the exercise of cognition, emotion, and imagination in the apprehension or constitution of aesthetic value can claim a philosophically more impressive heritage," (p. 326) disputing both the exclusion of cognition in the aesthetic experience as well as Carroll's historical argument for it.

Goldman's (2013) two main critiques of Kivy and Carroll's narrow view of the aesthetic experience are necessary to our understanding of the experiences constructed by culture wars aesthetics. What he defines as "The simultaneous and harmonious interaction and engagement of all these mental capacities is matched on the objective side by the interaction of formal, expressive, and representational aspects of the works appreciated,"[127] is the most effective description of the power of culture wars aestheticism. Much how Jay (1992) finds that aesthetic experience is constructed as a completion of reason, forming an ultimate literary absolute,

---

[125] Goldman, 324.
[126] Goldman, 326.
[127] Goldman, 329.

Goldman asserts here the same principle. The aesthetic experience's power lies with its ability to take the phenomenon of molding together material and immaterial reality and presenting it as a totalizing exposure to "the" truth.

A better way to materialize what this experience may look and feel like is under the umbrella of the law of the sublime, which Rancière (2009) describes as "the law of a disproportion, of an absence of any common measure between the intelligible and the sensible." (p. 6) Both Rancière (2009) and Jay (1992) cite Jean-François Lyotard in reference to this law, which presents us with an overwhelming power of sensation. A wholly insurmountable sensuous experience in which all sensible differences are negated, and instead "add up to one and the same thing: the dependency of the mind on the event of an untameable sensuous shock."[128] This is the final outcome of the intended experiences manufactured by culture wars aesthetics. Having separated and remolded material and immaterial reality into a single unit of truth, culture wars aestheticism constructs experiences of sensuous richness, intended to spark the needed emotional responses to inspire, frighten, or generally polarize its audiences.

By placing the subject of aesthetic judgment in the way of the object represented by political content being discussed, the aesthetic experience can be more fully realized in the way it's intended to. This is because, as Jay puts it of aesthetic judgment, "When,

---

[128] Rancière, "The Aesthetic Dimension," 6.

for example, I call a painting beautiful, I assume my taste is more than a personal quirk, but somehow expresses a judgment warranting universal assent. I imaginatively assume the point of view of the others, who would presumably share my evaluation."[129] Aesthetic judgment, along the same lines as the aesthetic experience, is meant to reshape material and immaterial reality into a single, uniform "truth" that can be argued for or against wholesale, and assumes a totalizing nature of the judgment being made. The assumption of a totalizing aesthetic judgment further reinforces the intended rich experiences that are meant to be constructed for audiences by culture wars aestheticism. Through the lens of totalized judgment, the receiver of the aesthetic experience is forced to either wholly accept or reject the complete reality that the constructed experience has designed for them. This "truth" borne from the remarriage of immaterial and material reality becomes no longer an aspect of understanding the object, which begins as a form of political content, and becomes the object itself. Political content becomes a mere vessel through which a culture warrior translates their noble and righteous cause of "the" truth and presents it to the dawdling masses.

To close this chapter, and to hopefully tie up this deconstruction of the aesthetics of the culture wars, I want to rebind them and clear up any final particulars to them that make them relevant to the larger subject of the culture wars at hand. In my understanding of it, the power of aesthetics is the

---

[129] Jay, "'The Aesthetic Ideology' as Ideology; Or, What Does It Mean to Aestheticize Politics?," 52.

power of this value called "beauty," which can also be called "goodness." This value holds so much power because of its ability, I believe, to realize the intricate differences between material reality, a reality of facts and objects, and immaterial reality, a reality of emotions, interpretations and cognition. These two realities are the dual axes that define the human world, thus making them an indispensable tool to recognize and make use of. Aesthetics can make use of material and immaterial reality in many ways, but it is how they are constructed in relationship to one another that gives them power over the human perception of both the world and themselves. In the first chapter of this book, I wrote about the development of tools at the top of the paleolithic era and their contribution to the development of culture. This is a good example of this power at play. While we can only retrospectively speculate, one could posit the power of aesthetics in the physical object of tools, which are the material cumulation of resources put together in a particular way based on the ideas of people, and giving them a certain value. This value could be pride, accomplishment or progress. It could just as well be disgust, anger or fear. It is my belief that aesthetics gives us the power to decide that value. And through the application of this value, the behaviors, beliefs and societies of the world develop. Aesthetics forms part of the core of the culture wars, as we have already discussed to some degree. Its ability to mend and twist meaning from objects and apply it back to them is the force that allows for the substance of culture wars debates in the first place, and thus understanding culture wars aestheticism is a necessary step in understanding both the fundamental makeup of as well as the means to win the culture wars.

Culture wars aestheticism accomplishes three central goals which we have actually already discussed. First, the aesthetics of the culture wars constructs a particular moral typology based on the ideology of the culture warrior. However, one thing to make clear of this moral typology which will carry over as a general theme of culture wars aestheticism broadly is that its construction of the world is totalizing and absolute. Whatever the particular "rights" and "wrongs" are, they are wholly "right" and wholly "wrong." The aesthetics of the culture wars does not believe in the partitioning of moral values or responsibility. This ethical framework confuses the rhetorical and practical use of a moral typology to the culture wars, which are by nature and by name, a *war*. Wars are rarely, especially based on their reputation, partitioned into sects of blame and wrongdoing that are accordingly punished to varying degrees. The aesthetics of the culture wars instead believe in some absolute moral law, regardless of what the content of that law actually is, which commands the whole of reality, and must be enforced as such.

Second, the aesthetics of the culture wars construct experiences through which participants will be exposed to the absolute moral typology in question in an overwhelming moment of shock and powerlessness. The aesthetic experience in the culture wars is constructed to present the aforementioned moral typology it has already created. It is predicated on an aesthetic judgment which assumes that its moral construction is warranting universal interpretation. This lens of aesthetic judgment forces participants to acknowledge its moral typology under the conditions that the culture warrior chooses, either becoming subject to its totalizing force or becoming its enemy. In either case, the predication of aesthetic judgment absorbs the participant into the aesthetic experience by force, making them inadvertently subject to the rules of culture wars aestheticism. Having done this, the aesthetics of the culture wars then presents its moral typology in what can only be described as an overwhelming fashion. It is through the complete subjugation to the "world" of the aesthetic that the culture warrior can ignite the deep emotions of their audience, and polarize them in some context towards the aesthetic. Using Goldman's broader view of the aesthetic experience, the complete exercise of the participant's mental faculties leads to a total immersion into the "world" of artwork, the otherwise fictional alternate reality of the work in comparison to our physical "real" world.[130] This covertly leads us to the third and final goal of culture wars aestheticism, which is to totally consume the participant in the immaterial "world" of aesthetic, completely detaching them from our material one.

Through the participant's absorption into the newly constructed reality of the culture wars, the final aim is to polarize the participant based on the moral typology it has presented to them. Through the lens of aesthetic experience, a culture warrior forces their participant into a position of overwhelming emotion and passion. The presentation of its aesthetic "world" in conflict with the morally opaque material one we

---

[130] Goldman, "The Broad View of Aesthetic Experience," 326.

live in serves multiple purposes for multiple audiences. For those averse to uncertainty, it can present a belief to cling to, one which presents uncomplicated moral goodness which must be protected, and evil which must be destroyed (think back to Dr. Anker's melodramatic political discourse). For those who are unmotivated to act on a political objective, it provides a spark of emotional ignition that can mobilize participants into acute political action. For those opposed to the political goals of the culture warrior, it serves merely as a signal of who the enemy truly is. Much as moths to a flame, the presentation of the aesthetics of a culture war attracts angry opposition who oppose, perhaps even outright hate, the moral typology constructed by the culture warrior.

Aesthetics plays a primary oft unheard and unseen role in the culture wars. It is the source of emotion and passion which moves the unmovable, and makes note of one's allies and enemies. However, one final looming question remains of culture wars aestheticism. In the distinction of a "material" and "immaterial" reality, the implication becomes that our world can be separated into these distinct classes, which concern themselves with a physical world of facts and objects which are amoral, or with the ideas and emotions we have about those facts and objects. This distinction, if analyzed long enough, may raise an important note: if the aim and behavior of culture wars aesthetics is to marry these distinct interpretations of existence and heighten the impact of the more immaterial interpretation, does that not make the base of the culture wars a war over arbitrary feelings? If the castle presented by Kant can be known both in the sensible of knowledge as an object of raw materials fashioned together in a particular way based on a plan as well as in the sensible of desire as a subject of awe, inspiration, pride and honor in all who are righteous and lucky enough to see it, does that mean a culture war over the castle is merely a bickering between whose feelings about it feel better?

The simple answer is yes. The culture wars are inherently tethered to the passions and cognition of the aesthetic experience. The presentation of culture wars aestheticism's moral typology is by definition an attempt to shore up feelings in an audience by different means (see chapter four) with a purpose in raising their political efficacy and mobilization. But the more interesting part of culture war aestheticism's intentions and methods is its subversive nature. I dare say even culture warriors are unaware of their engagement with the aesthetic experience in their attempts to build a coalition of supporters through their words and actions. Goldman gives Peter Kivy credit in saying he "may be right that most readers pay no such attention to structure as a whole and in itself, but this does not mean that they do not experience formal qualities while reading, as this cognitive engagement is combined with other aspects of the reading experience."[131] Much the same in social and political contexts, I believe we will find that neither participants nor culture warriors may be fully aware of the aesthetic processes and structural procedures they are undergoing when caught up in a culture war, but this does not negate that such

---

[131] Goldman, 328.

processes or procedures are happening. When we discuss (or perhaps more accurately, argue) about politics, we are not amoral robots concerned merely with some Pareto optimal legislative outcome determined by the particular details of a body's bylaws. At its face, political discourse is an emotionally charged battle between broader, cultural beliefs about the world and ourselves that cling to moral typologies that we construct and enforce via means of the aesthetic experience. As stated before, the factual "material" reality of our political and social experiences become, in the face of this far more personal and seemingly universal operative, nothing more than the technical nuts and bolts through which our abject "truths" will eventually become realized. This is what Rancière (2009) describes as the "aesthetics of politics," which he says "is not primarily a matter of laws and constitutions. Rather, it is a matter of configuring the sensible texture of the community for which those laws and constitutions make sense." (p. 8)

The aesthetics of the culture wars is the core of the culture wars because unlike the strategies of its warriors or the psychosocial foundations that define it, they are the first contact for all people into the raw emotional feeling that the culture wars, and thus what winning and losing them, will be like. They provide the personal-emotional value that the vast majority of this book's sociology and psychology jargon will never provide to the activists and individuals involved. In this sense, in spite of the seemingly arbitrary nature of culture wars aestheticism, it is very real. It is the difference between "happy holidays" being a menial phrase that is said from november to december every year, to the most important threat to the values of a nation and its religious people of our time. It is what separates the decision to refuse business from being a merely technical one to one that is bound forever to values that reject same sex marriage, and fashion those values as either being noble and true, or abhorrent and false. The aesthetic factor in the culture wars *is* the culture wars to most. Without it, any value they might have is hard to locate, if present at all.

And with such heavy weight, the aesthetics of the culture wars are necessary to the prospect of winning them. If the culture wars truly are tied to this aesthetic dimension, a dimension of deep passion and perception of the obscured material things of politics into symbols of oppression, freedom, fear, hate, love, joy, sorrow, and hope, then to win them one must tap into this dimension. Aesthetics is a game of cognition. Control how people's mental faculties are used, and towards what political content, and you have a stronger chance of emboldening their willingness to act. Through the active exploitation of the passion of aesthetic experience, the overwhelming exposure to content so charged with the ideas and feelings that will stir them to fight (or fight back), a culture warrior is given the opportunity to create perceptive victories and losses, even when the material world remains ultimately unchanged. This divorce from our "real" material world has a positive and a negative angle. From the positive angle, divorcing our "wars" from the material to the immaterial, where victory can be claimed for embarrassing an opponent in debate rather than killing them in a duel, can hopefully reduce any actual damage or death over our culture wars. We no longer march into our neighbor's territory and damage their possessions or their persons over whether or not they agree on our politics. However, the negative angle of this divorce is the obfuscation of the value and consequences of these culture wars in the realm of the immaterial. A total immersion into the "world" of culture wars aestheticism can mean total subjugation to a world of absolute truths which command the total destruction of one's enemies. It argues that compromise and coexistence is a nonsolution, that the potentiality of their freedom is a potentiality for future transgressions. Because of this threat, one side must "win," must eradicate the other. Hopefully, this means merely killing the idea of our opponents. But what happens if that fails? If we cannot reduce their ideology to dust until its irrelevance precedes it, how much further will a culture warrior be willing to go? The fear comes when we remember that the language of culture wars aestheticism gives a license to "destroy." This license may be vague, and one could argue it does not allow for physical violence. But excuse my lack of faith if I do not say it is impossible for some to interpret that license literally should the mission to destroy our enemy's ideology fails.

This is the final great concern with culture wars aestheticism. Even if its perceptive and immaterial battle is harmless, and in fact useful in reducing the physical damage of our culture wars, failure to deliver on promises that the evil enemy constructed by its aesthetics will be destroyed could lead to a roundabout explosion in physical violence. The tensions and frustrations and anger associated with our culture wars fostered by its aesthetics could result, then, in the decision that the word alone is not enough to defeat our enemies. The real challenge of winning the culture wars, if one does not want to see this result, is maintaining the immaterial precedence of the culture wars' aesthetics. Perhaps, by virtue of its nature, the aesthetics of the culture wars makes this outcome impossible. Perhaps that is the point of their existence. This much can only be assumed.

Chapter Six
Victory and the Culture Wars

In Part II's concluding chapter, I believe we must do a few things to effectively understand the culture wars better. First, I want to recollect our thoughts and reexamine our grounds for moving forward in order to answer the important questions of this chapter and Part II. In reviewing everything we've discussed, there are two major questions about the culture wars that we must answer, one of which is a given.

Q: What do culture warriors want?

A: *To win.*

Q: What is "winning" a culture war?

A: <u>*This*</u> *is our task and the task of Part II*

To answer that second question, I want us to review what we already know. First of all, we have designed a stratagem of the culture warrior. In its imperfect construction, the stratagem of the culture warrior is a collection of behaviors and habits we found the culture warrior to engage in with the explicit goal of "winning" the culture wars. However, more importantly we discovered an underlying theme about the stratagem of the culture warrior that makes it important to understand what winning the culture wars is. All the strategies we collected in chapter four are designed to engage an audience in the conflict of a culture war to polarize said audience and amass them as allies in it. This theme carried over into the aesthetics of the culture wars established in the last chapter. This is the first part of winning the culture wars I believe we can carry out as thematic to its existence. The culture wars are public spectacles, not private conflict. Like a performance, both sides play up the extremities and danger depicted by the performance in order to excite the audience. This exaggeration of a vague material reality is the other underlying theme of the culture wars. Carried over into culture wars' aesthetics, a culture warrior has the discursive ability to reconstruct "reality" into a single object which is understood on a totalizing level. This totalization of reality through means of interpretation is an underappreciated ability despite its frequent use. Its aim is to present political content in a particular way that elicits the emotions of the audience. A culture warrior takes political content, which recuses itself to a material position of opaque amorality, and exaggerates its details and effects until it becomes something new entirely.

The culture warrior takes advantage of multiple psychological factors in order to accomplish this effect of polarization. The reconstruction of a single, unified reality is not merely an attempt to create a narrative, but to inspire feelings of fear, hate, hope, pity, or vengeance in order to crystalize a bond between the audience and themselves that can be utilized as an allyship in later culture wars. This presentation of a unified reality is key to this effect because it optimizes the use of an audience's mental faculties without burning them out. In today's attention economy, human minds are not equipped to perceive of a reality that is disjointed and complex. The notion of varying levels of ethical and material responsibility and blame require an achievable, but not preferable, amount of mental work that one; would much rather be avoided. And two; does not satiate that human craving for the myth, the narrative, the story through which uncomplicated moral good and evil sit in opposition, through which their conflict can be resolved by a single, broad-reaching act of destruction. The aesthetics of the culture wars compliment the culture warrior's strategy by providing this cognitive-emotional perception of the political content in question. Through a reunion of material and immaterial reality as complementary to one another, subversively ordering immaterial cognition above material information hierarchically, the culture warrior creates said uncomplicated moral typologies that audiences can feed on, reducing the existential cost of joining in on their war.

What our synthesization of the stratagem of a culture warrior and culture wars aestheticism has elucidated for us is this concept of victory that can be tentatively applied to the culture wars. Victory in the culture wars clings to perception. Through the molding of perception vis a vis the construction of how one experiences a stimuli, the culture warrior creates a new reality that surrounds and encloses their intended participant. The capturing of a participant in this overwhelming ethos of "war," which ascribes danger in every outside thing which deviates from its self-ascribed perfect ordering of the universe, creates a vulnerable moment in which the participant will lash out, either succumbing to the narrative of the aesthetic, or rejecting it and polarizing against it. In either case, the culture warrior achieves their goal. Given the culture wars are a conflict of spectacle, part of their victory relies, too, in the establishment and maintenance of said spectacle. Much how effective activism brings attention to the most outlandish act to draw eyes and ears towards the intended political content, the culture wars aim to create spectacle of their conflict with the other side to qualify their claims of world-ending destruction imminent if one side doesn't destroy the other.

What we glean from this summation of what we have discussed at length in part II are three necessities that must occur in order to set the stage for a victory in the culture wars; An audience, a spectacle, and drama (in the form of deep emotional epitaphs espoused by our culture wars). Much like the stage play or the soap opera, the culture wars are a show, a performance through which the culture warrior as its actor-director will consume you in the world of its performance and you, as the audience, will become absorbed into it as a character. In this respect, the culture wars are the most groundbreaking performance in history, for their ability to convince the audience that the story is real and that they are all characters within it. The culture wars' command of realism to such an immersive degree gives it its power, and achieves its goal: to "win." Through the successful immersion into the culture war, the culture warrior "wins" the discursive battle. And while the war may continue, every minute victory counts towards its penultimate goal: the decimation of the evil other.

This brings us to our second question of winning the culture wars that has remained vague to us. Is there a means to win the totality of all culture wars? Do these issues or perceptions combine to create one single "war" which will be won through the gradual perception shift across issues? This question contains multiple fronts in order to best understand it. The theoretical front of this question of a unified culture wars is one which looks at the object of the political content which the culture wars are said to contain. This requires us, further, to question that content. Most descriptions we have encountered of the culture wars have defined them as a set of issues that harbor particular underlying themes. Themes of religion, political ideology, social cognition, etc. However, we have also begun to design an alternative description of the culture wars outside of these themes and issues, and instead focus on the underlying feelings and experiences that the culture wars create for participants and culture warriors. To what degree are the culture wars a set of issues of which there is a discourse about and to what degree are the culture wars the discourse itself? Our descent into definitional scrutinization confuses the larger subject of winning the culture wars, so we will entertain both notions to determine our answer.

First, let's assume that the culture wars are what people think they are, a collection of ideological issues related to religion and politics. The idea of a unified culture wars assumes, much as the culture warrior will assert through aesthetic and rhetorical claims, a universal reality, unified by a single ethical code and material configuration that binds every issue into a single political unit. The assumption is that is a single reality bound by the "truth" asserted by the culture warrior exists, and the culture wars are the result of fighting for that single "truth" against the false truths of other cultural and political groups. This can be further understood as Nikola Ilievski describes the broader subject of political integration, wherein he finds "the integration in a political sense results in building a political community, with the political units as its contents, through establishing same frame of rules, creating common institutions with the power of decision-making, and projecting an identity of the integrated community (instead of previous existing identities of the political units)."[132] We can align this understanding of the integration of diluted political beliefs into a single community and our understanding of the unification of political realities under a single banner as congruent processes that rely on one another. The process of developing a single "reality" all political actors must succumb to is related to, to some degree, the integration of multiple political units, however those units are understood.

This interpretation of the culture wars afford us an understanding of a unified culture wars as being the integration of a diverse political realities under a single banner of "truth" vis a vis the integration of political units into a single community. That literal act

---

[132] Ilievski, "THE CONCEPT OF POLITICAL INTEGRATION," 2.

of developing a community, which shares its institutions, customs, laws and facilities reinforces the values that said community espouses to believe. To understand this better, we must also take a look at a few theoretical approaches to ideology and how they conceive of a community's "voice" espousing its values. Much of how we have defined political allyship and community tacitly in this text has been through the use of rhetoric by a central actor or unit that then sees its rhetoric transformed into communal values or bonds that define the group the actor intended to create. This aligns with the social account of ideology that Homer-Dixon et al. (2013) found "typically placed a particular emphasis on discourse as not merely a passive medium through which pre-formed ideological content is communicated but as a central influence on ideological content itself."[133] This transformation of the rhetoric of those who hold power and those who, in democratic contexts, consent to their rule to the values of the whole nation presupposes a few ideas. First, one must understand whether or not a community's political context is, in fact, democratic or not. In a situation which it is, the assumption becomes that the "values" which are assumed are assumed by debate and discussion, the "best" among them, often meaning merely the best argued, have won out as that community's idea of the world's "ought to" as a collective. Other, non-democratic contexts, may vary. Some may assume the values espoused by the state as a mouthpiece are that community's values because of

---

[133] Homer-Dixon et al., "A Complex Systems Approach to the Study of Ideology," 340.

an ordinance from god or some supernatural force or figure. Some may assume the higher intelligence or better-equipped governing capabilities inherently make their espoused values those inherent to the community they rule for. These different political contexts are central to understanding this notion of unifying, and winning, a totalized culture wars.

In any political contexts, if we assume that the formation of a single unified political community presupposes the unification of the "values" espoused by that community, then to win the culture wars is to make, or remake the texture of one's political community on the cornerstone of one's set of values based on one's views on a set of political issues. Understanding the political context of a community allows us to investigate the credibility of these supposed shared values, as we can scrutinize whether a consensus was agreed upon, deliberated, enforced or brutalized into the psyche of said community. To avoid bias, even in the democratic context one must investigate the deeper context of the values espoused by the community so as to avoid a bias that assumes the aesthetic of democracy means that a community is truly free or equal. Practical applications of any political system may not mirror our aesthetics or our myths about them. In any case, this literal view of the culture wars finds that winning them may have more to do with the systemic and underlying institutional establishment of a community and what it espouses its "values" are, especially if those values drive material events such as passing legislation or enforcing laws.

Now let's face this second front of deeper theoretical obscurity. We previously explored a frightening possibility about the culture wars that sees them as the arbitrary battle of preferential cognitions of opaque material information. This view negates the assumption that the material world can be unified with its immaterial perception (whatever that perception may be), and identifies the perception alone as that which can be utilized for victory in the culture wars. If we deconstruct the culture wars as we have to their more atomized form, applying the aesthetic and emotional value they hold for us before any literal value of world-ending destruction or overwhelming evil, then is it so one can combine all these distinct feelings they're aiming to achieve? Henrik Kaare Nielsen speaks to this notion of a totalized aesthetics in finding that modern life is founded upon an aesthetic practice in the everyday lives of ordinary people that, ultimately, "is subjected to a stylized synthesization that makes it accessible to intense experience as well as focused contemplation. Hence, the complexity-reducing starting point of aesthetic practice in everyday experience paves the way for a special type of autonomous formation of meaning that can assume a multiplicity of forms."[134]

Nielsen's distinction is important because it does not assume a totalized aesthetics which achieves one final goal for the participant. One may assume, especially in the cases we have explored thus far regarding aesthetics, that to reduce complexity is to take the various material details of a situation and erase them. That to create the sanctified simplicity of

---

[134] Nielsen, "Totalizing Aesthetics?," 63.

aesthetic universality, one must, too, reduce the meaning that will come of the project of a totalized aesthetics to being this "oneness" that cannot be transcended or escaped. However, as Nielsen points out, "This structure of expectations can then be confirmed or challenged and reshaped in various ways in the encounter between a concrete artefact [sic] and an individual recipient's specific biographical ballast." (p. 63) The aesthetic experience itself can be more or less a stockpile that can be reflectively drawn upon from various angles, totality being nothing more than a technicality which crystalizes whatever conclusions the individual comes to afterward. As Nielsen put it, "The process of aesthetic experience is thus in its structure a constant exploratory movement between an object that cannot be fully determined and a universal concept that does not exist."[135]

"This general tendency to aestheticize is a prominent characteristic of highly developed modern societies," Neilson argues.[136] But this tendency has a root in something more than mere laziness. A root that is familiar to some of the social science research we explored earlier in this very work. He says "it is a question of the advancing process of individualization nourished partly by the amount of rights that is increasingly being extended to individual citizens ... and partly by the securing of the individual's material existence." (p. 67) Part of modern society's aesthetics beyond politics alone is an aesthetics of self-and-other, playing a strategy game in which the both the individual and society around them are

---

[135] Nielsen, 64.
[136] Nielsen, 67.

constructed in a particular way. This game, however, is exhausting. Especially if one entertains our notion of separating the aesthetic-emotional cognition from material information in drawing meaning, one may become hopelessly lost in this never ending spiral of parallel material "truths" that don't necessarily combine to create a uniformed reality that tells both the individual and society their respective "ought to's." Neilson posits the solution becomes, then, to aestheticize the community. Through processing the mental work of determining self-and-other in the framework of community, particularly those communities which the self is a member of or akin to, the work of identity becomes streamlined and more accessible.[137] This is parallel to our findings on rhetoric and social identification, where how individuals become themselves is often through the lens of how individuals become good members of their social groups and following the example group leaders give them.[138]

How does this help us understand winning the culture wars? I believe it comes parallel with our previous revelation. Our first, more literal interpretation of winning the culture wars found that it was related to the ability to reshape the texture of one's community. To literally change the makeup of one's society to one that symbolized, acted upon, and espoused the views of one side, one could say they "won" the culture wars from that sense. Identically, even in the more cognitive framework, to "win" a totality of the culture wars is to create a unified

---

[137] Nielsen, 68.
[138] Hogg, "Social Identity Theory."

community in part or in whole on the aesthetics of the "correct" side of a culture war. This construction signifies a unification of self-and-other thoughts that waters down the complexities of a disjointed reality and renders them obsolete in a more totalized, homogenous society that can be easily informed, convinced and marketed to of the same things. This is, in part, Nielsen's issue with this aesthetic unification.

This tendency to aestheticize politics implies the obvious danger that the associated appeal to individuals in their capacity as passive clients and consumers marginalizes the role of the critical, publicly reasoning citizen on which the democratic process subsists. Likewise, the central position of the media in the societal reduction of complexity gives nourishment to a 'reversal of reality' in which it is not processes and relations between citizens but rather the medial representation as such that becomes the guarantee for, for instance, the reality and the perspectives of a political project.[139]

In either case, I believe we have discovered the art of winning a totality of the culture wars necessitates an imaginative totality of the community with the self. Along the same view of our aesthetic unification of "truth" in chapter five, to construct the community in such a way that its rendition of the culture wars are this totalized project ensures that both institutional, issue-based politics and the more

---

[139] Nielsen, "Totalizing Aesthetics?," 69–70.

cognitive interpretations of those systems and issues
are convinced of this absolute victory.

　　To sum, as I fear we may lose some clarity in
our exploration, the distinction we have just made is
that which finds both the issue-based approach to the
culture wars *and* the deeper, culture
wars-as-discourse approach to them finds that a
unification of community through its aesthetic,
cognitive makeup and the literal makeup of the
institutions and laws that make the community (or
more appropriately the society), one can achieve
victory in the culture wars. Change the way people feel
and see their society and then change the issue
priorities and institutional responses to them and you
have more or less achieved the victory you so seek.
This finding cuts at what I believe to be the last
distinction we must make in this chapter and in Part
II. Since chapter five, we have separated what we
defined as "material reality" and "immaterial reality"
as two spheres through which make the world. One
sphere takes its literal, material objects and measures
them, replicates them, alters them, plans with them
and exploits them to create new, material realities
that impact the world and vice versa. The other sphere
approaches this same material "stuff" for a lack of
better term, and pulls from it something else. This
something else is what I have generally referred to as
meaning. If it is a material reality that I am sitting on
a chair, it may be an immaterial reality that it is a
good and noble chair, brought to rest my butt on by
the grace of an almighty overseer who is rewarding me
for my acts of heroism and intelligence. I have a right
to this chair, and my relationship to it as a material

thing becomes something more, something I see not with my eyes but with my mind. My imagination stirs a series of feelings that will drive the way I behave in reference to and around this chair. This distinction was made in the last chapter to determine how aesthetics contributes to winning the culture wars. And while we explored the separation (and later reunification) of immaterial and material reality to make such a distinction, I want to close this chapter and Part II with a deeper exploration of the relationship these two things have to one another that makes winning the culture wars what it is.

As I stated before, we have already begun to cut at this relationship in this chapter. Among our most pertinent takeaways for Part II, the distinction and marriages of material and immaterial reality, I hope, remain ingrained the deepest. For, to win a culture war, one must make use of these two realities with or without the knowledge or acknowledgement of doing so. And it is their ultimate reunification that creates the final sensation of "winning" the culture wars that I wish to make note of here. If immaterial victory in the culture wars is changing the way society feels and thinks about the culture wars, and material victory in the culture wars is changing the way society acts and reacts to the culture wars, what is their summation?

First, totalized victory in the culture wars is absolute. It dominates and destroys. It either wholly defeats the other side, or it doesn't defeat them at all. Furthermore, its references to the state of affairs; to the weather, to best color nail polish, they all becomes subsumed into the absolute of the culture wars. Our earlier question of total victory itself is subjectively answered in this assertion. Yes, all culture wars can be won. Because all culture wars are part of the absolute culture war. What this results in materially can be a rather callous disregard for safety, strategy or life. The absolute domination of an absolute evil is the absolute goal of an absolute good. Absolutely. I digress, this value of totality is, in fact, what makes totalized victory in the culture wars totalized. Returning to Neilson's "Totalized Aesthetics," he refers to the role of mass media in the modern, aesthetic age of politics and how its "concretizing reduction of complexity also makes use of cognitive and moral discourses, but a basic operation of aesthetic practice, the transformation of intangible relations and structures of meaning into tangible ones."[140] Much how the earlier discussion of streamlining of identity work of self through the simpler network of the community totalizes those two's dichotomy, Neilson's point highlights a similar effect in (particularly in the case the of media) how views of the world are streamlined from their ambiguous reality to a reduced simplicity.

The key theme of this simplicity is its moral clarity. The absolution of totalized victory reflects notions of moral clearness explored in the previous chapter that justify a particular set of political behaviors. For one, these behaviors materialize as speech. In CNN's first presidential debate between Joe Biden and Donald Trump on June 27th, 2024, Former President Trump described Biden's job as his successor in no shorter order than the worst that there has ever been.[141] Trump's colorization of the Biden

---

[140] Nielsen, 69.
[141] "READ."

administration is one of absolute disaster from which the US could never return. "Look, he's the worst president in the history of our country. He's destroyed our country ... If he wins this election, our country doesn't have a chance. Not even a chance of coming out of this rut. We probably won't have a country left anymore. That's how bad it is."[142] The absolute nature of totalized victory in the culture wars, in a prospective lens, is one that clearly notates a dichotomy between two absolutes. That, in this case an electorate, we must choose between obvious moral values which have obvious material effects. There is no room for opaqueness or uncertainty in the absolution of totalized victory in the culture wars. Such uncertainty undermines everything totalized victory represents: a rejection of our fear of uncertainty, establishment of clear-to-define emotional cognitions of reality and forms of justice for defying them. Absolution in the totalized victory in the culture wars is a semantic and aesthetic glue which binds together totalized victory's janky parts together. It smoothes totalized victory's rough edges and illogical connections with an assertion of "the" truth that arbitrarily binds together incompatible immaterial cognitions and material facts in an emotionally satisfying way. The promise of absolute victory over an uncertain and insurmountable evil gives us a reason to switch off our reasonable objections to totalized victory and its outcomes because we are promised a sensation of emotional satisfaction.

---

[142] "READ."

Finally, it is these material aftereffects we must discuss, for politics is not merely a set of cognitions about the world, but what material actions humans take to realize those cognitions. I believe, at our present moment, these effects make themselves quite clear. For instance, the Oklahoma superintendent of public instruction exacted an order requiring the instruction of the christian bible and the 10 commandments in public classrooms. The superintendent, Ryan Walters, made it explicitly clear that adherence to the rule was compulsory, and that "immediate and strict compliance is expected."[143] This policy plays into the culture wars on religion in America and public schooling. Superintendent Walter's strategy seems to be using his power as a public official to force what is in his mind as a morally objective and materially correct material into classrooms and into the minds of young students at a time when they are their most impenetrable, undercutting alternative education which might make a less obedient populace. His memo directly states this when he says "This is not merely an educational directive but a crucial step in ensuring our students grasp the core values and historical context of our country."[144] This rhetorical reflection reveals Walters' true feelings, and implies the full expected effects, about this policy: The bible (and the 10 commandments) are an inherent truth, and have a direct influence on the makeup on the United States of America as a community and an institution and

---

[143] Speakman, "Oklahoma Schools Are Now Required to Teach the Bible and Ten Commandments," para. 4.

[144] Walters, "Immediate Implementation of Foundational Texts in Curriculum," para. 2.

should be taught and seen as such, period. This absolution negates all other views of these materials and the political reality of their mandatory instruction. The christian bible is a document rooted in history, including American history. But both it and christianity's influence is highly overstated by zealous christians who incorrectly feel they have more of an inherent right to the privileges and powers of the US government than everyone else. Their need for total domination, based on an incredulous reading of God's commandment to spread his gospel to all nations on earth in Mark 13:10,[145] has evolved into a political objective. However, in the view of Walters and religious allies, this distorted quest is a righteous march towards "the" truth. Its absolute origin necessitates an absolute enforcement. Including punishments against defection from his perfect truth like suspending the licenses of teachers who refuse.[146]

Totalized victory in the culture wars is wholly uncompromising. Much like how if all reality becomes bound together by a single "truth," such truth cannot be defied or fragmented to account for the different experiences and beliefs they produce for others. It must not share its victory in a coalition of winners, but alone. We have discussed this feeling before in a different context. In our unambiguous disinterest in co-partisan cooperation, the fourth designation of a culture war, feelings of uncompromising, too, appear. Our finding then was that this disinterest in cooperation was the result of the construction of

---

[145] Various Authors, *Holy Bible*.

[146] Kingkade and Parra, "OK Schools Head Vows Sanctions for Teachers Who Won't Teach the Bible."

absolute "truth," and the moral goodness that comes with it. I am right and good. Therefore, my getting what I want is right and good as well. All other options are wrong and evil. They cannot happen. This simplification of the logic we have already explored is rematerialized in the totalized victory in the culture wars as simply being my getting what I want. My policy objectives, as a reflection of the absolute truth and material benefit of them, have been achieved. Furthermore, they have been achieved alone. This can be better understood in the context of bipartisan legislation on Capitol Hill in the US.

In order to understand the issues of bipartisan legislation, one must understand the implications of bipartisan legislation. To sign on to legislation approved by a(ny) member of the "other" side, that which is supposed to be evil and against all we represent, is an admission that their view of the world and their ambitions for it have any degree of merit. Today's political climate, consumed by myths of good and evil in their purest forms, consumed by the culture wars which have dictated that politics is a battle between absolute truths, could never allow such possibilities to exist. And conceptually, they don't. We explored this earlier with the concept of the slippery slope in the stratagem of the culture warrior, which we found acted as a way for culture warriors to temporarily ally with "the enemy" under the pretense that it was necessary to pass needed legislation without negating their role as "the enemy." This is possible, in part, to the American public's feeble knowledge of the US government against their general political knowledge. Comparing 2023 data from the

Pew Research Center to a 2022 survey conducted by the Annenberg Public Policy Center at the University of Pennsylvania, while over 60% of Americans knew which party was in control of congress,[147] less than 50% of Americans can name the three branches of government.[148] This slight disproportion in knowledge is exploited in the case of bipartisan legislation, as while a considerable chunk of legislation sponsored in congress is, in fact, bipartisan,[149] obfuscation of that knowledge allows members of congress to sponsor and support such legislation while simultaneously denouncing what such legislation represents; That being, a negation of the absolute truth value which the culture warrior has previously established and is trying to win the culture wars on. To negate such a value is to negate the culture warrior's victory. But the material reality remains that broader coalitions are needed to pass legislation, or major electoral victories. These, too, can be achieved by rewriting the electoral system in a way that benefits one party absolutely, encouraging that disregard for compromise.

Totalizing victory in the culture wars masks material complexity with aesthetic and rhetorical simplicity. In a world of millions of various details, factors and contributing issues to our political problems and systems, human beings tremble in fear not merely of the uncertainty such complexity represents, but in open disgust of it. Complexity

---

[147] Gracia, "What Americans Know about Their Government," para. 5.
[148] the Annenberg Public Policy Center, "Americans' Civics Knowledge Drops on First Amendment and Branches of Government | Annenberg," para. 5.
[149] O'Brien, "The Lugar Center and McCourt School Release Latest Bipartisan Index Rankings for Congress."

represents mental work needed to accomplish tasks. It requires a deep breadth of attention, resources and relationships to create and maintain experiences that will sustain societies and alleviate their potential issues. But this work can be taxing, and not always rewarding in the superficial, totalizing way humans desire to see it done. Because of the nature of compromise, of strategic political maneuvers and ally ships, the complex nature of politics as a work infuriates the ideologue. The ideologue, represented in our case by the culture warrior, conceives of a world of total values and absolute victories. To win, to destroy the enemy, and to dominate institutions with their antithetical good ideals. Especially for the layman, who has no time to worry about the cogs of politics after a long week at their own work, navigating the already frighteningly complex landscapes of their own careers, their social and romantic relationships, parenthood, taxes, bringing food home etc;

These complex details that create the political realities we face are simply too much, and too dull, to constitute the victory that a culture warrior and their followers seek. Simplification is a necessary step in achieving the full feeling of winning the culture wars. Nielsen told us about this in reference to the absolution of totalized victory in the culture wars. In that same vein, a totalized victory's absolution comes with a cognitive simplicity that highlights the absolution and provides most importantly a feeling of satisfaction in victory. The happiness of knowing we defeated our enemies, saved the country, and are imposing an objectively better way of life into the system that will branch out for generations, influencing the people of the future under our better ontologies, is a much more satisfying thought than merely allying with "the other side" temporarily in order to achieve some small victory that contributes to the greater cause. As a matter of fact, we look down at those who do this work as being idyllic and utopian. Their tireless effort and willingness to cooperate with anyone capable of helping them effectively impact an issue in some way is lamented as a weakness, as "giving in" to the evil other and their progress is downplayed as meaningless or corrupted by the influence of the other side. The culture warrior's victory is, instead, repurposed merely as a single act, or simplified to its least complicated form, even if a series of complex factors made it possible materially.

This simplicity is more satisfying to imagine; it is easier to say Americans simply "defeated" Donald Trump in 2020 by showing up for Joe Biden at the polls when many people remained polarized about either of their candidacy and a lot of work was done to convince democratic voters to show up and swing unaffiliated voters in Biden's direction or to discourage them from voting third party or for Trump. The work is a complex reality stilted by American voters' reservations about either candidate, instead attempting to appease Democratic culture warrior's fantasies about Biden and their party as being more clearly morally and materially correct and recognized as such. It gives the party an energy it can use to further accomplish its political goals and energize voters in their base, giving us the typical "honeymoon period" that occurs after a new President is elected and their party wins a majority in the congress.

We have attacked this question as to whether the culture wars is more material or immaterial in its inception from just about every angle. We have discussed its aesthetics, the strategies which culture warriors approach them from and have attempted to understand concrete policy actions with the aesthetic-emotional cognitions we invent about them. I believe, from this analysis and more to come, that we can say the nature of the culture wars is one which sits in between material actions and reactions and immaterial cognitions, with immaterial cognitions leading the way in what material actions may or may not take place. Allow me to explain;

I have attempted to tacitly sew the seeds of emotional cognitions leading the direction of material behaviors the further we've delved into this question with the hope of arguing this in the finality of this chapter: the ultimate aim of the culture wars in its victory, and the ultimate aim of politics as a result of its fusion with the culture wars and its victory, is to achieve a certain feeling. The policy actions we take, those we vote into or out of office, decisions by our supreme courts and executives to expand or shrink their power, international war and diplomatic peace; all of it exists to preserve and protect a sensibility our nations, our people, we, have about ourselves. We conceptualized humans in their evolution in part one. The nature of our social groups, why we form them, how we self actualize through them, and the themes from that definitional chapter carry over now to this. Our groups or tribes, defined both as nation states and as political parties and the endlessly splintered factions therein, create a certain feeling of self. This feeling of self, in order to self actualize and mobilize, creates an idea of goodness that it associates with self. To be me is to be a good person. To be a good person is to be me. The antithetical evil we invent in others is part of that process, an exaggeration of other-ness that comes from the fear of the unknown that a more tribal human species would have had about unknown humans and what their intentions are with the "us" that is both the self and the tribe.

Our politics reflects this setback in our psychological growth. The need for the evil other, the antithetical evil to our inherent good, the villain to our hero, it makes us in an unfortunate way. The rationalization of this emotional cognition of self and others, however, has long been obfuscated by a cult of reason born from the Enlightenment, a period defined by its discovery and excessive use of material facts to argue points of view. The human discovery of material reality in its rawest form cursed us to this cult of reason, wherein all things are ceaselessly argued down to their most minute material definition. But what material facts, as we have already discovered, have always fallen short of explaining and arguing, is the certain feeling of being human. The lividness at a messy, underprepared political debate. The joy at the victory of a contentious election. The despair at the realization of a legislative loss. All these political material realities, of course could be tied to a long series of chemical emotions in the physical minds of people, based on the physiological and psychosocial material realities they inherent and experience. But that literal explanation does not provide us with the full view of a life. Despite what the cult of reason clings to, our lives are not merely a series of material things happening in our field of view to compute. In our minds, in our feelings, it is so much more. It is a moral struggle we have invented, a display of color and form that rather than merely being observed by humans like a camera, is enjoyed and enamored and interacted with. Our emotional cognitions are themselves material realities, yes. But to lose the emotional aspect of them is, in fact, to lose the human aspect of them, forever damning oneself to an eternity of endless computation.

This, unfortunately, means that we create culture wars. And those culture wars consume us and our emotions. And their victory becomes a necessary emotional state which we will achieve through our understanding and execution of material information. We will make connections, lobby, vote, campaign, pass legislation, issue opinions and executive orders, and fight wars. We will elect strongmen and expand and shrink our supreme court and our presidency. We will fight civil wars and erect new governments, write constitutions and rewrite the material texture of our society. But we do not do these things, not always, for the pure reason of it. The reasoning, the logic we employ, we do so to ensure we achieve the material outcome we want. We achieve the material outcome we want, we achieve what was always most important to us: the feeling of victory. The catharsis that signifies meaning to us, reinforcing our moral typologies and our commitment to the "right side" of history.

This discovery brings us to the end of part II. It also opens our questions for part III. If it is the case that we will do these things, what does this say about our Democracy in America, and around the world? If it is the case, as I argued in the introduction, that the culture wars are growing in their importance, becoming more and more the way in which we engage in our politics, will our politics become the absolute dichotomy that the culture wars make it? These are the fears of our time. That democracy is backsliding. That voters in the US as well as in the world are embracing the delusions of culture warriors turned presidents and prime ministers. The other question is this: with this rising prominence of a discourse of moral clarity, absolute certainty, and the destruction of an evil other, how do we defend from it? From this monster that lives in us, finding an element of darkness in every face we see that we do not recognize.

I believe the answer will be to investigate not merely ourselves, and not merely the institutions we create. I believe we will have to interrogate the discourse itself. We will have to face the culture wars, and in its eyes we will see ourselves reflected. In the certainty and the heated passion of the culture wars, we will find fear and anxiety. And we will be forced, then, to reconcile these things with ourselves and with each other. Let us begin.

Part III

The Culture Wars and Democracy

Chapter Seven

In Contempt of Freedom

"I believe there is a style of mind that is far from new and that is not necessarily right-wing," wrote Richard Hofstadter in the November 1964 issue of Harper's Magazine. "I call it the paranoid style simply because no other word adequately evokes the sense of heated exaggeration, suspiciousness, and conspiratorial fantasy that I have in mind."[150] His essay, *The Paranoid Style in American Politics,* and its primary thesis will serve as a parallel realization to ours in this, the third and final part of this book. Hofstadter's "paranoid style" is tantamount, I believe, to the materialization of what we may call a culture warrior identity and the politics of the culture wars, before they had such an identification. Hofstadter's concern was in the wake of Senator McCarthy's looning rave against communism corrupting every echelon of society in the midst of the Cold War, in the same month that President Kennedy was set to be assassinated by a communist-sympathetic spy. "The paranoid style," Hofstadter writes, "is an old and recurrent phenomenon in our public life which has been frequently linked with movements of suspicious discontent." (para. 2)

His historic account, which explored conspiratorial paranoias around Illuminism and Masonry at America's birth and Jesuits infiltrating

---

[150] Hofstadter, "The Paranoid Style in American Politics," para. 1.

American society just before the breakout of the Civil War, extrapolates the deeply moral outrage at the exigence of these ideologies and their application in American society, further creating the fear of this unseen evil around every corner, in every church, stealing every elected office.[151] The moral vitriol as part of this conspiracy theory aligns with our hypothesis of the culture wars, as does the construction of a battle to destroy this evil. This is where we will pause, to close in on this subject of the evil other, and the abject totalitarian reality constructed by the culture warrior established in Part II, in order to understand what the struggle between these various absolute truths becomes in the context of Democracy. We will also return to Hofstadter throughout Part III as a reference point.

We've discussed the construction of the evil other before in various contexts. Drawing back from Dr Elizabeth Anker's *Orgies of Feeling,* political agency comes from the characterization of political actors through the lens of heroes and villains. The moral economy she describes that comes from this characterization which reinforces the goodness of the hero (ourselves as the culture warrior or their ally) and the evil of the other (our immediate enemy or opponent) and the injuries they've inflicted on us (everything from their religious practices to bills they pass in congress to their mere existence, depending on our own level of extremism). But this discursive construction of the evil other, coupled with the aesthetic reconstruction of a uniform "reality" which backs up both the trueness and goodness of our belief

---

[151] Hofstadter, paras. 6–19.

system, justifies our hatred, dehumanization of and potential violence towards them as our enemy on merely a descriptive, cognitive level. There is a psychological background, too, to the otherization of outsiders, which further strengthens our concerns about the culture warrior's disregard for democracy, and in particular for the freedom of others as invalid. Finkel et al. (2020) explores what they call political sectarianism in America, a heightened version of the same tribalism we associate with our politics and which we have used as a parallel to our development of the culture wars, claiming that "cold feelings toward the out-party now exceed warm feelings toward the in-party. Out-party hate has also become more powerful than in-party love as a predictor of voting behavior (2), and by some metrics, it exceeds long-standing antipathies around race and religion (SM)."[152]

This finding is nothing new. Having explored tribalism in a very limited way, we understand that through the creation of the collective, which realizes itself (and thus provides its individual members to realize themselves) as good and as having true beliefs, so follows an unfortunate miscalculation which assumes all other groups as having false beliefs, and if they become overbearing or antagonistic, evil. This has carried over in our exploration of political parties as well. However, what makes Finkel et al.'s exploration pertinent for this chapter, is in fact its adoption of the moralized nature of political sectarianism's belief structure. The misobservation of the evil other is not merely a psychological mistake, a

---

[152] Finkel et al., "Political Sectarianism in America," 533.

maladaptation from the recesses of the unevolved human mind. Instead, they argue, "Whereas the foundational metaphor for tribalism is kinship, the foundational metaphor for political sectarianism is religion, which evokes analogies focusing less on genetic relatedness than on strong faith in the moral correctness and superiority of one's sect." (p. 533) This moralization, alongside the emergence of traditional otherization and aversion in an unholy trinity of ideological delusion, creates an attitude about political opposition that Finkel et al. theorize will cause "political losses [to] feel like existential threats that must be averted—whatever the cost." (p. 533)

This is textbook culture wars theory. And it aligns too with the feelings of "other" Hofstadter warns of in the wake of McCarthyism in the sixties. He writes, "the modern right wing, as Daniel Bell has put it, feels dispossessed: America has been largely taken away from them and their kind, though they are determined to try to repossess it and to prevent the final destructive act of subversion."[153] The moralization here aligns with Finkel et al.'s observation and with the deep moral feelings that signify the culture wars to us. Furthermore, they elucidate meaning in how we can understand both the situation Hofstadter was observing then, and what it does as a representative for how culture warriors and those sympathetic to them feel about politics now.

In the political struggle for cultural supremacy, the sort of material representation of an immaterial

---

[153] Hofstadter, "The Paranoid Style in American Politics," para. 20.

and deeply emotional struggle between ways of life, to see a country adopt much—perhaps any—of the lifestyle, political, social or religious artifacts and physical ones therein that represent those cultures which are not our own is an act of subversion and invasion. In a very roundabout way, we see a fundamental observation of human tribalism reasserted here, if not magnified: to not see the world reflect only that which I know and understand is to see the world reflect a threat towards it. Finkel et al. continues, "partisans nevertheless vastly overestimate such differences. They view opposing partisans as more socially distant, ideologically extreme, politically engaged, contemptuous, and uncooperative than is actually the case."[154] The delusion takes hold at a certain point, and the culture warrior simply begins to invent an idea of their opponent in their head, obfuscating the real human person across from them. The moral reconstruction of their culture—and them as its purveyor—has led to the othering that dehumanizes the group. Together, the collective imagination of outsiders will produce Finkel et al.'s final requirement for sectarianism: aversion. The moral lessering of and dehumanization of other cultures complete, the feelings that accompany them arrive, and the cycle reinforces itself. A new imaginary will be constructed to account for new information that contradicts it, and a deep cognitive dissonance is abound to deflect any admittance that the in-group's inherent rightness or goodness is exaggerated or made up.

---

[154] Finkel et al., "Political Sectarianism in America," 534.

This relationship with others and how it causes partisans to behave towards them, nonetheless politically, is at odds with ideas of pluralism that are part of the American conception of Democracy. American Democracy has been the embodiment of many political philosophies of the freedom of cultures to exist and participate in the governing faculties of it as a nation-state. Over time, some have gained more traction than others, some have been discarded, and some are posited but never truly lived out. Among them, theoretically, is the principle of pluralism that defines the outer edges of American freedom. Pluralism as a philosophy of free society proposes the possibility of multiple ways of life merely coexisting, all alongside one another in shared society and shared governance, none to ever take precedence over any other. Pluralism can be as superficial as the existence of multiple religious entities and as deep as the allowance of a plurality of value systems that contribute to society,[155] but it is its political iteration that backs up the American idea of freedom in this sense. In a truly pluralistic society, the multiplicity of social groups within a nation maintain the same right to engage with the political engine of said nation through various means, including the right to vote, to protest and engaging with members of the elected legislative assembly. (sec. 1.1)

The reason I claim what we have discerned about the ideology of the culture warrior is at odds with this principle, and thusly at odds with Democracy to a degree, is precisely because there is reason to believe that a culture warrior, steeped in the

---

[155] Hoffe, "Pluralism and Toleration," sec. 1.1.

delusions of their ideology, will come to feel that those other groups are not deserving of these rights or privileges, and are privy to taking political action to rescind said rights as a result. This finding is vindicated by those of Graham and Slovik (2020), a piece of research we explored in chapter two which found that American voters' care for democracy effectively ended if it meant defecting from politically supporting a candidate within the same party identification as them.[156] Moreover, as we previously explored, partisan voters unfairly apply scrutiny when the other side backslides on democratic values, but may not be willing to engage in the same kind of scrutiny with their own party.[157] This is the best example of the "delusion" part of this ideological delusion which I have referenced. This is the extent, I believe, of the outer edges of the culture warrior identity. So trapped inside a 1x1 chamber of self-affirming biases and enough pseudo-factual information to back up the culture warrior's cognition, their field of view of the outer "real" world becomes totally obstructed. In this echo chamber, constructed both in the digital world and the real one, the culture warrior becomes aware of that which only concerns their bias. Information which does not affirm is not accepted, it is flawed. Returning to Finkel et al., we understand now this religious connotation associated with sectarianism, and why it is stronger and more devoted than base tribalism or party loyalty.

Furthermore, this heavily influences how the culture warrior treats others in a material way as well.

---

[156] Graham and Svolik, "Democracy in America?"

[157] Graham and Svolik, 393.

Beyond merely their voting habits reflecting a callous disregard for democracy as a form of government, partisans express support or antipathy for certain issues to a deeper level. Graham and Slovik (2020) have more ingrained findings beyond the baseline rejection of democracy at a partisan cost in a complication in their results. They say, "While all undemocratic positions impact a candidate's vote share negatively, the magnitude of that effect ranges from 10.2% to 16.1%.23 Respondents most severely punish candidates who want to prosecute journalists (16.1%) and ignore court rulings (14.1%). Respondents are least sensitive to candidates who endorse gerrymandering (by 2 seat, 10.6%) and suggest that the governor ban protests or rule by executive order (10.2 and 10.5%, respectively)."[158] Certain actions, I think we will find, have a certain discursive value placed on them by culture warriors as leaders of their partisan factions. They notate which actions (i.e., prosecuting journalists versus endorsing gerrymandering) are more-or-less acceptable responses to the exaggerated evil of the other side. This helps guardrail what actions may be too large to reframe. Ignoring a ruling by a court and acting erroneously towards it may simply be too obviously authoritarian to fool even the most dedicated partisan. In such a situation, one would rely on the hope that a partisan's hatred for the other side is so strong action taken in defiance towards a court is acceptable, a risk that isn't necessarily worth staking one's political life on.

---

[158] Graham and Svolik, 402.

As stated in the previous chapter, as well, certain political acts are simply more interesting than others. As creatures of emotion and cognition, certain acts may be easier to adopt into our normative story-oriented understanding of the world. Aesthetically, we can stitch the ruling of a court and the passing of a law into our understanding of the world with its perfect moral dichotomies and sweeping, absolute acts of villainy and heroism. The same cannot necessarily be said about the complexity of, for instance, zoning, which may come across as bland and not worth the effort to learn about. Furthermore, work which may be more complex and detail-oriented in nature, like lobbying and information-sharing on Capitol Hill, may simply be reduced into a more aesthetically pleasing version of itself which can be repurposed to fulfill partisan desires of perception.

I want to return to our aesthetic colorization of the culture wars, particularly in aspect to their victory, and contrast it to the pluralistic notion of political and social tolerance and what that means in a society. "As pluralistic democracy cannot arise nor continue to subsist without the mutual toleration of otherness, tolerance is, at least in the weaker form, a fundamental principle of modern states," writes Hoffe.[159] However, he continues, tolerance is achieved in both a passive and active state, both necessary to the realization of a truly free nation.(sec. 2.2) In its passive form, there is a baseline acknowledgement of the "other" as a being, regarding its qualities as a person, understanding their background as one which

---

[159] Hoffe, "Pluralism and Toleration," sec. 2.2.

produced them, and how it might create their faults. But it is the evolution of this acknowledgement into the more active form, a "candid recognition of the other and otherness ... grounded in the dignity and the liberty of every human being."(sec. 2.2) This active form doesn't merely recognize the material fact of another's existence, it assigns it a particular value. In fact, it assigns all "others" a particular value of inherent dignity, allowing for liberty. This value, at a baseline, is a symbol of this evolved tolerance, and requires its passive state in order to become what it is. The passive state of tolerance allows for the recognition of people as being that, people. The humanization of others negates the dehumanization of sectarianist culture warrior mentalities which aim to reduce the human other into an amorphous evil other. This amorphous shape that represents our opponents is easier and more appealing to accept because their annihilation becomes justified. To strip the rights of someone who is less than in a deep, dehumanizing way is not only acceptable, it is good. Abstracting the details of their lives which might make them more appealing or more real to us, which occurs in the recognition that what makes them who they are is merely the same thing as what makes us who we are: their emotions, the reasoning used to justify them, and the physiological and psychosocial conditions which produced them and their experiences. The aesthetics of the culture wars play the heaviest hand in erasing this nuance, removing any details that might influence us to believe a person is a person, thus further negating our ability to think a person is grounded in dignity or worthy of liberty.

Instead, the culture warrior identity in its sectarianist delusions does what we have discussed before at length. It justifies the utter obliteration of a people under a blanket of ethically two dimensional claims about moral clarity and abject reality. Let's use Richard Hofstadter's observations in 1964 to realize this myth a bit further:

The enemy is clearly delineated: he is a perfect model of malice, a kind of amoral superman—sinister, ubiquitous, powerful, cruel, sensual, luxury-loving. Unlike the rest of us, the enemy is not caught in the toils of the vast mechanism of history, himself a victim of his past, his desires, his limitations. He wills, indeed he manufactures, the mechanism of history, or tries to deflect the normal course of history in an evil way. He makes crises, starts runs on banks, causes depressions, manufactures disasters, and then enjoys and profits from the misery he has produced. The paranoid's interpretation of history is distinctly personal: decisive events are not taken as part of the stream of history, but as the consequences of someone's will. Very often the enemy is held to possess some especially effective source of power: he controls the press; he has unlimited funds; he has a new secret for influencing the mind (brainwashing); he has a special technique for seduction (the Catholic confessional).[160]

---

[160] Hofstadter, "The Paranoid Style in American Politics," para. 31.

Separated by some sixty years, Hofstadter recognizes the same delusion of partisan ideology we see today in the sectarian nature of the culture wars. The totalizing control and overwhelming power of the evil other is recognized in the uncontrollable events of modern life, of life at all. An arrogant assumption is made that all the development we have made in technology and science and reason has made us gods, when in reality it has made us better animals. That arrogance produces the delusion of the culture warrior and their partisan followers. And their response to the abstracted and layered nature of the material world and the infinite immaterial cognitions produced to understand it is the utter rejection of it. Finkel et al. finds Americans, particularly strong Republicans and Democrats, discriminate on job applications and scholarship recommendations based on partisan affiliation.[161] When it comes to the issue of electoral representation, they find that such a democratic function is undermined by the nature of partisan electoral politics, incentivizing politicians to only represent same-partisans.(pg. 535) Sectarian partisans are more susceptible to exploitation and manipulation done by social media accounts posing as a same-partisan, and the tendencies of sectarianism undermine the very function of government competency, "Members of Congress increasingly prioritize partisan purity over the sorts of compromises that appeal to a large proportion of the population, a tendency that creates legislative gridlock."(pg. 535)

---

[161] Finkel et al., "Political Sectarianism in America," 535.

A deep contempt of freedom is fostered by the sectarian nature of culture wars identity and engagement in said culture wars. Freedom itself loses its pluralist angle, and instead becomes merely a vacuum within which sectarian partisans, culture warriors, "the paranoid" as Richard Hofstadter calls them, can express their beliefs based on their experiences alone. Freedom is reduced to being in a paradox with the abject "truth" invented by the culture warrior, for to submit to this totalizing force and posit its predeterminations is to be free, and to oppose it or demean it as being exaggerated or to restrict it or regulate it is to be an oppressor. The freedom of others to posit their own ideas, to live their own lives in the way which they have determined is best and provides the most material and immaterial emotional value, is to allow the misguided fools of the masses to idiotically stumble through life, destroying all of the objective good our superior faction is unearthing and creating.

This is obviously not the case, creating such a paradox. Under the unification of immaterial and material reality under "one truth," true freedom expressed in part by pluralist society and democracy becomes obsolete. If it were the case that all things combined to create such a unified "truth," then what would freedom mean? Precisely, it would mean nothing. To be free to submit to the authority of a single unified reality, bound together by some arbitrary and all-encompassing rules, is not to be free at all. The culture warrior's delusion creates an environment defined by its antipathy to the freedom of others by discursively rebranding it as not freedom at all, but as an attack on themselves. Using the strategy of victim-claiming, wherein the culture warrior reconstructs the "war" at hand as being one which they are the overwhelmed and helpless victim of, they are capable of writing off the liberty of others as utterly invalid, justifying both implicit biases against others as well as explicit political actions taken to restrict, lessen, or otherwise remove such freedoms for others.

But I want to take a moment to pause and reexamine Hofstadter's criticism of this mentality and clarify a point he makes so that its relevance is maintained for our purposes. When creating a sense of the "paranoid" sensibility about their evil other, he writes "The paranoid's interpretation of history is distinctly personal: decisive events are not taken as part of the stream of history, but as the consequences of someone's will."[162] His misalignment with the right at his point in history, overtaken by the paranoia of what we would probably call the mentality of the culture wars led by a few prominent warriors of the sixties, comes from the simplification and personalization of historical events as being the result of the will of a single individual or group. He correctly contrasts the more complex "stream of history" with the singular will of "someone" to dispel this broad-sweeping notion of aesthetic simplicity, something we determined is part of accomplishing that feeling of victory in the culture wars. But I want to clarify, and I believe this was the intended meaning, that the "stream of history" is not merely random acts which remain perpetually out of the

---

[162] Hofstadter, "The Paranoid Style in American Politics," para. 31.

control of mankind. Thinking of potential retorts to Hofstadter's critique, it's possible one may downplay the complex reality of existence by arguing the fair point that societies are not mere accidents. The social fabric of collectives which constitute themselves by the technical makeup of their political institutions are very much the intentional results of the pointed efforts of individuals. But it is for exactly that reason that the two dimensional conspiracy which concerns the paranoid culture warrior reduces the will of many people into a single person or as being totally the same across a group. This reduction in the wills of tens of hundreds of thousands is an intentional reduction of the value and necessity of compromise, even within groups which maintain the same position. The myth of the totalitarian collective, particularly in the instance of politics, obscures the fact that many within a group might share a vaguely similar, if at all the same vision for a totality's political or social outcome. But this does not mean that said collective's will must be virtually the same or represented perfectly by the will of a single individual. "The stream of history" in Hofstadter's language is merely shorthand for the painstaking work of politics, which we have discussed before, and its unique ability to take a disjointed and ambiguous reality, composed of a same material basis which informs an infinite potentiality of experiences and subsequent beliefs and desires, both socially and politically, manifested in the form of political collectives or actions.

Imagine if you will that reality is an infinite forest. It is grounded in the soil, a shared material reality that remains largely itself over a prolonged period of time. From this shared soil, many countless trees all sprout up. Each tree is a different cognitive interpretation of reality, an ideology, a way of life. The trees, in large part, are based in some way or another, far-or-closely separated to the soil below. Each takes its own form, however. Each grows different branch patterns, producing its own shade. Every tree is taking nutrients from the soil below, and in some cases the roots of each tree share nutrients with those of other trees, or have roots which entangle or overlap. All the same, the trees are *not* the soil. And the soil is *not* the tree. As well, neither a single infinite plot of soil or a single tree could possibly be defined as a "forest" all its own. Each needs the other to constitute the full reality of life. What we may call the delusion of ideology in the culture wars, which we have explored throughout this chapter and the antipathy towards freedom it has produced can be understood from this analogy.

If I sit under the shade of a particular tree, and I recognize this tree incorrectly as being the entire forest, I am mistaken. While it may be the case that my tree is, in fact, grounded in the soil that is the base of the forest, I have lost all the former facts we have just asserted. The mistake, I believe, is rooted in my point of view. When I limit my vision to the edge of the tree I am currently under's shade, I refuse to see the other trees around me, and acknowledge they, too, provide shade to other people. What occurs, then, in societies which attempt this pluralist, liberal democracy is that I hear of other trees and I am lost. Whatever value I have given my tree, my "reality," has been stolen, and an existential crisis ensues. A bitterness is instilled, and I become fearful that the acknowledgement of other trees in the forest is an attempt to cut mine down, leaving me with no shade, no meaning, at all.

But this is not the case. Rather, every tree is part of the forest. They are parallel to one another, each drawn from different experiences and beliefs. It is not the case that all facts and interpretations combine to create this single truth, that all roots come from or mend together into a single tree. The tree comes from a shared soil with other trees, other ways of life, other ideologies. Together, they make the forest. It is this recognition that nobody's tree is *the* tree under which all of humanity will enjoy the shade that liberates the mind from itself. Contempt of freedom dies as acceptance of the forest—reality—is neither just a set of facts or a single cognition of them. It is both. And the aim of an effective pluralistic democracy, which accepts and endorses the freedom to sit under which tree's shade one feels most comfortable under, is the constant work of politics we refer to. This is perhaps the most difficult part of this argument. Because I am not here to tell you that said work is done, or ever will be. In fact, I don't think it ever is. America's Constitution posits the existence of a "more perfect union" within its preamble. This line means a lot, and has been made to mean a lot more, in the face of political battles and culture wars. But what I think we may come to find is that a "perfect union," in all of its totality, is not explicitly mentioned for this exact reason. There won't ever be a perfect union. A forest won't ever be a single tree. But a forest can be made more beautiful and better protected. Weeds and invasive species can be removed. Trees can be cut down when they get too old or too unsafe to sit under. A shared constitutive reality, based on a shared material reality, can be made through the tireless effort of those engaged in the exhausting work of politics. This work will require compromise, but it will also require serious questions, questions of ethics and shared morality, to be answered by a pluralistic collective.

A pluralistic reality, and its realization through democracy, is not an admission that "everyone is right." This exaggeration misses the very legitimate concern that, as Hoffe denotes, "becomes visible in the form of the ideologically neutral state. It is reproached with relativism and even nihilism, because it does not even acknowledge certain very general values as binding and is held responsible, therefore, for the crises of meaning and orientation which threaten contemporary industrialized societies."[163] This threat is created when the neutral state simply allows everything, creating an anarchistic environment which abolishes the neutral state altogether, unable to maintain its own existence let alone hold anyone accountable for breaking the shared agreements of society as those agreements are seen perhaps merely as guidelines, not rules. Even within the context of a relativist and pluralistic agreement on rights, privileges and norms, the imaginary of these agreements does not negate their binding nature. They are ways we feel about the world and ourselves, but those feelings are not just empty voids which temporarily make up our minds and

---

[163] Hoffe, "Pluralism and Toleration," sec. 1.2.

hearts. In the fires of passion, our ways of life, especially those we have had to debate, argue and fight for both alongside and against others, must be treated with the same concrete respect they would be if our imaginary about totalizing universal truths was correct. Furthermore, collective social and moral agreements maintain a right to punish those who refuse such agreements and take actions which significantly undermine them. One may have the privilege to feel and think that an invasive species should be allowed in the forest of reality, but if their espousal of this feeling or their behavior because of it causes a material damage wherein the invasive species has, in fact, been let loose to damage or undermine the health of the whole forest, the invasive species must be removed. Simply accepting it because it is a part of the forest is not an acceptable course of action.

The ultimate challenge to a free society, which I believe democracy as we understand it best preserves, is not some foreign dictator or evil other in the wrong political party. It is ourselves. Our perfect "truths" create visions in our heads of a single reality, bound together by its virtuousness and moral clarity. But this myth exaggerates and reduces the full sense of reality as a shared series of constructs, based more-or-less in the same material reality which remains stagnant regardless of its perception. The modern struggle for democracy is the modern struggle of life, in a way. To overcome our own inhibitions and the delusions they inspire in us. To reconcile our feelings as an immaterial reality which is inexplicably intertwined with, yet totally removed from a shared material reality all the same. And then, from that point, to constitute collective agreements on who we are and where we stand relative to those who may feel and think different things about that same material reality. How to govern from this, how to write the law, protecting the political freedoms which will serve as the basic infrastructure of the whole of humanity's broader social and cultural freedom. And the greatest struggle of all of this, is to accomplish these tasks with a humble reconciliation of our own supremacy as nothing more than a feeling of self-efficacy rather than a great and righteous truth that we have an obligation to enforce.

It is the failure to accomplish this task I want to turn to next. As we have explored before, the outcomes of the delusion of the culture warrior in rejection of a larger, more whole conception of reality which encompasses the parallel interpretations of those who reside inside it can range from an attitude towards our invented enemies to flat-out undoing the work of democracy in the name of our righteous truths. But at what point does the evolution of the delusion of the culture warrior become violent? More pointedly, when does the language of war which constitutes the culture wars become literal? We posited this question in chapter five, worried that such descriptive language could be misinterpreted if the enemy's ideology is not defeated in the "marketplace of ideas." If their ideas pan out, and we still yet refuse them as evil and wrong, is there a point at which our language and rhetoric of being in a world-shattering battle with them becomes the inspiration of extremists and fanatics? I also believe this brings up an interesting secondary question about the nature of the culture warrior identity worth exploring: are culture warriors inherently extremist, or can they be legitimate political actors, engaged in legitimate political discourse?

Chapter Eight
A Discourse of War

This question of the rhetoric of the culture wars creating an environment that justifies and encourages political violence is rich in detail. In this chapter, I want to explore how language in the culture wars, which we have discussed sporadically throughout this book, necessitates and justifies various forms of violence, creating an environment where violent acts are acceptable and defensible. This requires us to ask questions that will define what constitutes violence specifically, to what extent, and to what end does the language of the culture wars create this violent atmosphere. Furthermore, I want to investigate how language creates extremists from culture warriors, how one's identity becomes tied to this act of violence as something that is acceptable, if not encouraged. This will also force us to reconcile something we have been rather unclear on throughout this book: is the "culture warrior" identity inherently extremist in itself?

To guide us through our first set of questions, looking further into how language creates an environment of violence, I pull from Riner (2023)'s poignant *Language and Violence*. She says, "perspectives that place violence outside of language rely, I contend, not on a misrepresentation of violence, but on a misunderstanding of language."[164]

---

[164] Riner, "Language and Violence," para. 7.

This misinterpretation, she continues, is the result of the normalization of a "referentialist ideology of language,"(Riner, 2023, para. 7) which reduces language to purely its symbolic and representational value. But she argues that language does more than simply make noise alongside the "real" experiences we have and feel, rather constituting those experiences altogether. This point treads familiar ground, returning us to our binary of material and immaterial realities. Inasmuch that the power of language to constitute our experiences is one and the same with the act of immaterial cognition of a material reality. Through language, we can assign and reassign certain values to events and objects, giving those things more or less power to us as the ones which perceive them.

Riner (2023) continues that language and violence as an experience can be inherently tied because of the emotional experience which violence may create for its victims. Using Susan Hirsch's account of testifying on trial for the 1998 bombing of US Embassy in Kenya that killed her husband as a powerful example, she writes, "Theorizations of violence can benefit from this perspective on language that recognizes its experiential and often inchoate qualities, rather than perceiving it as inauthentic representation dichotomously opposed to faithful experience."[165] An abstraction of violence from language and vice versa fail to recognize what bonds the two together, that emotional quality that surrounds violent acts. This is reminiscent of our conclusion in chapter six, which found that victory in the culture wars is less about the enactment of some

---

[165] Riner, para. 8.

policy goal, or even the act of undermining and establishing a new government, but through the achievement of a certain emotional catharsis that signified meaning to the individual. The power of language is that it decides what is and what is not through the convention of speech and linguistics. Our previous discoveries about the achievement of particular feelings in politics, about the aesthetic reconstruction of the meaning of political content so that one may justify a certain reaction to it, all fails without this recognition that none of these objects is possible without the discursive power of language to recognize and assign meaning to them.

But this is just the first angle of language and violence. If this power is so great, to what extent does language and violence interlope to create the experiential qualities of violence that we're concerned about? Riner (2023) actually argues "On one hand, meaning itself can be violent."[166] It is not merely what language *does* that can be violent, that can cause harm, but the language itself that causes harm in irreparable ways. Part of that violence comes from the mere fact that language has such power as a system through which meaning is invented and assigned. "Discourses are frameworks that inform what we know," Riner writes, "including shaping what we can know. They are controlling in that they erect structures of meaning that we cannot necessarily see around."[167] If the power of aesthetics is the power of perception, then the power of language is like the enforcing body for that perception. To discursively

---

[166] Riner, para. 10.
[167] Riner, para. 11.

create the perception of an aesthetic absolute and apply it to our political opponents is to condemn them to self explanation, creating an environment where they are what we say they are, and our situation is what we say it is. Meaning can be assigned and united across time as well, wherein language can employ chronotropic (meaning referring to or from a particular moment in time) conventions to create a certain kind of recognizable meaning to a population. The use of antiquated terms of patriotism and endearment or vitriol and disgust "equates conflicts across time and space,"[168] bringing conflicts across time together as one, continuous struggle. This allows us to create a historical account of our culture wars in particular, through which we can create from our otherwise short-term policy and social clashes a sort of grander, long-spanning battle between good and evil which transcends time.

Language can be pointedly weaponized not merely in the ways it creates meaning, but in the way meanings create it. Hate speech, recognized by most legal systems in the developed world, is one way in which this can be the case. Riner (2023) finds,"The semantic meaning of the words used does not render speech injurious on its own. Hate speech cannot exist in a vacuum."[169] Rather, what constitutes the injurious effect of the language of hate speech is the existence of a framework for violence that the speech is a part of. The social and historic contexts through which injury is intended, and the speech, rather than orchestrating the violence through meaning, is the channel through

---

[168] Riner, para. 12.
[169] Riner, para. 22.

which such violent meaning is meant to be espoused. Furthermore, the violent nature of this speech is what it does to incite or excuse physical violence, once again referencing the larger framework of violence which the speech is a part of.

This environment of violence and the language which is created and sustains it uses speech and its ability to assign or change meaning in various ways that support "the distinctly modern form of perpetual violence in which we now live."[170] In the investigation of language as a sustaining force of structural violence, Riner (2023) explores how language creates discourse that can determine and control the kinds of people there are allowed to be, and within what normative framework ought they be expected to live their lives in.(para. 28) This should sound familiar, as we discussed in our exploration of the victory of the culture wars, the necessity of controlling the way people are (allowed) to think of themselves in the context of self-and-society so that certain views on how the world "ought to" be are normalized into the psyche like a branding iron. Through this reorganization of the popular consciousness around one preferential set of values, the culture warrior is given an authorization then to reorganize, too, the sensible texture of society through its institutions. Popular consciousness having now adopted its normalized preferences, the culture warrior is allowed freely to change institutional powers in ways that systemically affirm the culture warrior's ideology and values alone. "...structural violence extends perpetually beyond the actions of individuals who are

---

[170] Riner, para. 28.

concealed behind anonymous institutions," says Riner (2023), "and who recede into the past and disappear as the violence continues."[171] The lasting legacy of bending culture around you and your beliefs is one which reverberates across time and space. To influence thought in such a way that you change the way people feel, and thus how they think, about themselves in relation to society and vice versa is not merely an exercise in persuasion. Using language, the culture warrior can force their opponents into a position of vitriol and existential crisis. This is intentional, the culture warrior's language is meant to convey images of absolute dichotomies that either erase their enemies, another form of linguistic violence that accompanies literal genocides in their ability to erase cultures and people by erasing their language,[172] or force them into the existential darkness of not being right, good, and thus not real. Through this crisis, the culture warrior can then convey an invitation to defect, discreetly brutalizing the identities and characters of people into formatted versions of themselves. The safety and security of this new righteous identity creates a chain reaction, wherein the whole group follows the example of the leader, punishes defectors, and further fights for the group's dominance and supremacy in an invisible battlefield. A lasting legacy of violence as institutions and people are changed in ways that crystalize the culture warrior's ideology as "the" truth indefinitely, until the next can come along.

---

[171] Riner, para. 29.
[172] Riner, para. 24.

The direct facilitation of violence is a particular ability of language that comes in various forms. The predicate for language that calls for violence is the belief, and linguistic overstating, of group homogeneity. The false belief in group homogeneity may stem from the categorization of groups around social prototypes—a series of fuzzy interrelated attributes that are pressed together into a single, tangible description of different types of people. Michael Hogg's (2023) concern brought up with this practice, however, was when the prototype preceded the person. In this case, we begin to see this set of attributes *before* we see the ridged edges of their personalities, likely because to do so would directly contradict the mental effort put into creating a mental image of who they are by smoothing over the specific details of their character to mend together their basic group-related attributes. This reduction of individuals and their groups results in false belief, and overstating, of homogeneity in both in-groups and outgroups.[173] This effect, they argue, is stronger among those who hold what they define as "essentialist" beliefs. What this means, they say, "[is that they] think groups' characteristics are immutable and historically stable and therefore conceptualize social groups as sharply separated and unalterable."(pg. 4) The result is a belief, as well, that the two as social groups are utterly incompatible, correlating with justification for prejudice and inequalities between the groups. Furthermore, coming down the actual language of it, they find that when describing the "desirable" qualities of the in-group

---

[173] Baele et al., "Lethal Words," 4.

compared to the out-groups' "indesirable" qualities, they use more abstract language which essentializes the out-group negatively, and the in-group positively.(pg. 4) Taking what we know about social identity theory and conflict, it's no surprise that groups will both gloss over the complex details of human character to essentialize a person as being a series of interrelated traits and being bad for them. But, it is the employment of abstract adjectives to describe this relationship that enriches our understanding of language and violence. Rather than the specific, quantifiable qualities of our goodness or badness that we focus on, it is apparent that we may instead confuse those qualities, merely to broadly describe ourselves as "good" and our opponents as "evil." We appeal to the emotional quality of our difference, the moral rift between us that, when seen and felt, differentializes us to a polarizing degree, and intentionally so. Furthermore, returning to the stratagem of a culture warrior, we do this to polarize outside audiences. We want to exemplify a difference so clear and so abhorrent that not to join us is an inexcusable act of treason. In this way, we don't just justify violence against our obvious opponents, but also against spectators who don't immediately and unquestioningly side with us.

Riner (2023) finds that, "Through analysis of the microdetails of talk, researchers have examined the linguistic negotiation of moral stances by which people position themselves and their and others' agency in relation to acts of violence ... These moralities, moreover, can shift even in the span of one interpersonal interaction."[174] Both speech and the way we speak it can change agency in violent acts in ways that shift from act to act. It is used to disseminate responsibility or negate it altogether, artificially moving and removing meaning in ways that are convenient to the speaker, keeping their own ideological purity free from risk, while shifting the value of and agency behind violent acts to other, human or non-human acts. And it is for such a goal that this constant flux of moralities occurs, as well, to maintain the righteous purity of the good and right self, while shifting the responsibility for violent acts that have occurred because of the self onto something else; whether it be an outside, non-human agent, some encompassing force that gave the individual "no other choice," or merely deflecting the responsibility on some other actor and making it appear as a kind of necessity, as being a retaliation or a prevention, and not merely a senseless act of violence predicated on our own mistaken preconceptions about our political opponents.

A particular situation this applies to is the July 13th, 2024 assassination attempt of Donald Trump. At a rally in Pennsylvania that evening, a lone shooter opened fire at the former president, grazing his ear and killing one attendee.[175] While the shooter's motivations seem ambiguous, and likely apolitical, a twofold debate broke out in which some leftists denounced the condemnation of a possible instance of political violence as appeasement to a would-be

---

[174] Riner, "Language and Violence," para. 34.

[175] Colvin et al., "Trump Survives Apparent Assassination Attempt, One Attendee Killed, FBI Investigates | AP News."

dictator who himself has tacitly enabled and supported violent acts, reframing the potential to kill him as more of a retaliatory right of an oppressed people. In this instance, despite the shooter being a registered Republican,[176] Leftists defending the violence have associated with him likely in response to Republican lawmakers blaming the shooting on President Joe Biden's existential rhetoric about the former president. Furthermore, the shifting moralities about political violence described by Riner (2023) occur in this instance, as leftist language about the assassination attempt have shifted away from the actual event and the shooter responsible for it, and have instead deferred responsibility onto Trump (and tacitly onto all Republicans by association) in an attempt to reject the notion that their in-group would be capable of such violence without it being warranted.

This also aligns with Baele et al.'s (2023) finding that "Victimization narratives connecting violence and conspiracy are of course well known to scholars of radicalization."[177] Similar to the strategy of victim-claiming, this finding means that the act of self victimization couples with the act of a conspiracy plastered against an out-group meant to reveal a covert, less directly injurious action meant to keep them as the victim in a state of oppression or subjugation.[178] Yet, to leftists, this insidious conspiracy against them is true. Donald Trump and

---

[176] Biesecker et al., "Trump Assassination Attempt: What We Know about the Suspect | AP News."

[177] Baele et al., "Lethal Words," 8.

[178] Baele et al., 6.

the Republican party under him (if not before him) intentionally victimize them out of spite for their way of life and the political freedoms that enable it. I think this may not necessarily *not* be true, as Republican policies over time, most certainly under President Trump, tend not to benefit non-republican voters as congressional districts are drawn in such a way that only incentivizes representation of the party, not the full district. Examples of this might include the infamous transgender military ban,[179] a rule that cut millions of federal dollars from Planned Parenthood,[180] or the deployment of federal officers to US cities and continued threat of federal intervention to forcibly shut down Black Lives Matter protests.[181]

The only "issue" so to speak of the leftist retort is the moral characterization of it. In one account of his supporters by a Reddit user in 2023, "Trump supporters are either incurably ignorant or just plain evil."[182] This brings us back to the aesthetics of the culture wars and their attempt to construct a single, moral "truth" from material reality and our emotional-aesthetic cognitions of it. The left's conception of the Republican party, especially under Donald Trump's leadership, is one of pure malice. They are evil simply because they are evil, and want "us" all in a camp somewhere or dead. This vivid description of Republican policymaking takes the

---

[179] "The Trump Administration's Transgender Military Ban."

[180] Ollstein, "Trump Administration Issues Rule to Strip Millions from Planned Parenthood."

[181] Superville, Sullivan, and Morrison, "Trump Threatens Military Force against Protesters Nationwide."

[182] TheRealSnorkel, "Trump Supporters Are Either Incurably Ignorant or Just Plain Evil."

material realities of Republican policies, like those mentioned above, like the appointment of federal judges and supreme court justices that are more sympathetic to a conservative legal philosophy, and processes it through the cognition of emotion, the core of the human experience of consciousness. Through this cognition, Republican rhetoric about an equally existential and evil left and their policy actions is taken with the Republican policy response as a contribution to their highly moralistic dichotomy. But of course, the failure here is the assertion of a cold and maligned Right wing, one in which is evil for the sake of evil or just plain stupid. Somehow, Republicans are *not* the outcome of their experiences and cognitions. They are not fallible and imperfect people, afraid of life and more afraid of death, forming their own cognitions of the world based on what information they may know and inventing the rest so that they may not have to live in fear of what they don't. The unified truth and righteousness of the single reality constructed by leftists pits Republicans as being the antithetical pure immutable evil to their pure incorruptible good.

But we have strayed from the subject of this chapter a bit, and have a second question still to answer. Taking from our previous example, I want to explore the nature of the culture warrior identity and ask; is the identity of the culture warrior and the language associated with it inherently extremist? Does what we understand about the discourse of the culture wars imply an innate radicality to those who identify with it as a motivating force behind their actions? We begin this investigation with a tricky realization, as it is the case that "The narrative surrounding extremism is controlled by those in a place of power and privilege, as they dictate to society what is normal and what is extreme."[183] Just how Baele et al. (2023) explored how language created extremists inwardly, how it reflected the views and behaviors of extremism, we must too understand how language creates extremism externally, how language builds the extremist from its point of privilege. The primary issue with the external definition of extremism is that it is inherently tied to the political power a "majority" holds within certain institutions, and how they use it to create a discursive environment that controls the meaning of what is both "normal" and "extreme." Furthermore, the delusions of political ideology are likely to take a place in this conversation, as to conceive of one's views which contribute to their self efficacy as the fringe of society, and potentially dangerous, is ideological suicide.

As Williford (2019) finds, "Assuming the law should regulate extremism, the road to implementation is complicated not only because of First Amendment protections, but also the effects of mislabeling individuals or groups as 'extremist.'"[184] Using the American legal system as her example, no strict definition of "extremism" has truly been adopted, instead American legal institutions choosing to protect and clearly define what *can't* be held against groups based around certain beliefs in a very negative liberty sense. There is a definitional vacuum left in which individual organizations, from civil rights

---

[183] Williford, "Blurred Lines," 937.
[184] Williford, 938.

groups to the Federal Bureau of Investigation, all create their own terms of what is and is not "extreme," and by extension what is and is not "normal." More than this, these splintered definitions are likely to be siphoned through the respective organization's mission statements,[185] making each definition tinted through the cognitions of those who sustain each organization and its leaders as the ones with power inside of them. Certain overlapping themes develop definitionally, even if the principled origins of each definition diverge based on ideology, such as "exclusion from the mainstream." But again, the missions of all those who differently define extremism must be treated as unreliable narrators. From our previous example, and taking into consideration what we know about the poor perceptions political affiliates have about one another, if the left's general view of Donald Trump is extreme, their view of anyone who supports him will be considered extremist and out of the norm. This both controls what the "norm" is and unfairly and unrealistically centers it around what those who identify with the left have experienced and believe, as well as denotes anything outside of the siloed experiences of those who identify as politically left as not only inherently outside the norm, but also inherently extreme and possibly prone to violence. This might be considered "unreliable" because of what we know about partisan cross-perception: it is deathly unreliable. Partisans regularly misconceive of each other as being far more extreme, uncooperative, and contemptuous than is actually the case.[186] Even the act

---

[185] Williford, 939.

[186] Finkel et al., "Political Sectarianism in America," 534.

of extrapolating the cross-partisan definitions may cause issues, as Williford (2019) notes that definitions like "unwillingness to listen to an opposing point of view" would essentially cover everyone, thus making us all extremists.[187]

Rather than attempting to define the ontological nature of extremism, collectives tend to define "elements surrounding extremism, such as violence..."(pg. 940) What might make an extremist in the political and legal sense is the advocation, plotting or execution of violent acts in order to circumvent the democratic project and force through political outcomes. This definition may be more functionally useful for us as to define extremism at all in a ontological sense may simply be the result of our delusions and biases. There is much reason to believe that, in this case, no one is a reliable narrator. Therefore, to find that "while a person would not be punished for their abstract beliefs, they could be punished for depraved motives,"[188] is the next best step, and the reason many of us, including me, argue against the defense of political violence by leftists against Trump. To simply believe something means nothing. To espouse a belief is something more. With the weight of language behind a belief, it can evolve into behavior that influences systemic developments or cultural construction. To behave in an explicitly violent manner, to evolve a belief and how one espouses it to be unapologetically pro-violence as a means to achieve one's ends, is something wholly different. Baele et al. (2023) expounds on this;

---

[187] Williford, "Blurred Lines," 940.
[188] Williford, 941.

In extremist language, descriptive assertions abound that the meta-ingroup and the meta-outgroup are fundamentally distinct, together with normative claims that the ingroup works toward enforcing this separation, which we call the "purity gap." The more obsessed by the purity gap an extremist group becomes, the more violent it becomes, as evidenced in an increasingly exclusive language containing more and more action verbs denoting themes such as eradication or cleansing.[189]

This kind of language, and the violent acts which follow, creates an environment of acceptability—necessity, even—in which an individual otherwise acting within the "norm" becomes extremist through the provocation or execution of said violent acts. But we must pause. We have still yet created a discursive definition of what is normal and what is not? What is the basis of this definition? Can it be considered a "safe" definition if we have just determined there are no reliable narrators who can determine what is either normal or extreme?

I believe as far as definitions go, one which underpins what is normal and what is extreme along the environment around extremism, and not the thing itself, may be the best functional definition of extremism we have. Not to say that defining extremism based on its environment alone, the actions it produces, the discursive acceptance and

---

[189] Baele et al., "Lethal Words," 10.

justification of violence, purity and ideological distinction and segregation as symbolic of this environment, is perfect. This definition still skimps on what makes extremism extreme by merely allowing societies to share the discursive weight of defining and the best agreement made in this collective framework is one which focuses more on actions and the elements of belief that create particular, injurious actions. Furthermore, this mere act of labeling can have dangerous side effects that inadvertently cause individuals disassociating from their normal peers and collecting with others under said label, creating extremist organizations that may act out the violence we accuse them of harboring, bound together by our defining them.[190] To name something or someone, and furthermore for the subject to respond to this act, is "an act of submission to the authority that has conferred the act of hailing and as such is a 'violent act that subjectivizes individuals and indoctrinates them into the norms and power relations' of their social order."[191]

This, unfortunately, circulates us back to the original point. The act of naming has immense power that creates ideas of what is acceptable and what is not. It invents an idea, too, of who is the "norm," and the power that holds, and who is the "extreme," and thus the subservient fringe subjected to the will of the norm. By defining normality and extremity in terms of the facilitation and acceptability of violent acts, we can avoid the messy and unfortunate conventions of discursive definitions of who is and is not allowed to

---

[190] Williford, "Blurred Lines," 944.
[191] Riner, "Language and Violence," para. 18.

exist, including those that inspire people to adopt violent ideologies, and instead criticize their acceptance of the environment of violence within which they justify violent acts as an acceptable way to force political goals through societies.

With all of this in mind, then, is the culture warrior identity inherently extremist? Earlier, we described the development of the culture warrior's identity as being the result of an aversion towards uncertainty. We have also defined parts of the culture warrior's identity as being that which aesthetically reconstructs "truth" into a single, definable object that merges and hierarchically orders immaterial cognition over material information, as part of their larger rejection of a disjointed and complex reality. This same effect is accomplished in fashioning their own identity in reflection, collecting a series of acceptable prototypes others have invented who share certain interests or characteristics with them and internalizing them as a part of who they are. None of these things fit our working definition of extremism. It is normal for people, when confronted by the void in their lives, to run away in fear. To take what little they know and inflate it into an immutable truth, a weapon against the darkness of the moral void, and to invent patterns and emotional truths as a response to fill in anything their exaggerated information cannot explain. To develop beliefs based on experiences which are simultaneously predicated on and the foundation for other beliefs is part of what it means to be human. Even, unfortunately, when those beliefs are exclusionary and hateful. The view, for example, that transgender women are not "real" women and should not be allowed to use restrooms assigned for this arbitrary category of "woman" may feel hateful and non inclusive. But to define it as extreme or treat it with the kind of vitriol that extremism is given is unwarranted.

People with this belief, despite what the delusions of ideology persuade, do not regularly invent it from a place of pure malice. This fantasy serves no purpose other than to exaggerate and invent our own fantasies which justify their utter annihilation. The need for violence and actions which reflect this need are part of what should make extremism extreme. We are an evolved species. Murder and abuse are the political and social tactics of a species with smaller brains and less functional societies. So, if someone's belief is (or becomes) that transgender women are not only not real, but all innately sexual predators and groom on children and should be abused, jailed, killed and harassed for said delusions about them, to label it as extreme and treat it accordingly is appropriate. It creates an environment where violent acts are necessary, just, and acceptable in order to achieve a political and social goal. The argument may be, however, that the previous "less extreme" belief is an inherent precursor to the first. This is a valid response, but I think it oversimplifies the relationship between a belief that trans people don't belong in a particular bathroom and that they should be harassed or killed. There is obviously an underlying relationship between the two: a rejection of transgender identity as being valid or real. However, this relationship is purely correlative because of either belief's basis in the rejection of transgender identity. One does not innately necessitate the other, nor does one inherently lead to the other. The development from an exclusionary belief to a violent one requires not merely the underlying pretext which constitutes both beliefs but the normalization of violence as a necessary act in society in order to accomplish the goal of the underlying pretext. In short, both have a similar feeling about a stimuli, but the extreme one moves beyond merely feeling it, and acts upon the instinct to squash it.

The language of the culture wars creates an environment that can evolve into one that justifies and necessitates violent acts. The ethos of "war," the victimization associated with the identity and tactics of the culture warrior, and the need to eradicate all aesthetically unsatisfying materials which contradict the simplistic universal truth of the culture wars are the building blocks of a dangerous political discourse which can, and will, turn bloody if someone doesn't get their way. We see this exemplified across time regardless of political origin. Nobody is safe from their own fear and hatred of that which they do not yet know. Yet, if this animosity has constructed itself out of our own minds, into political and social acts that could topple democratic governments and eradicate the trust between people, what could possibly be done to aid us from our own ineptness? This will be my final argument, and the last chapter of part III and this book. We will investigate the nature of our affiliations, and come to understand how we may be able to transcend their grasp on us without rejecting all those experiences which have defined us, and will define us in the future. For it is not those experiences that are invalid or that must be abandoned. But it is our petulant clinging to them and what they have taught us in the face of the moral void ahead of us in this terrifying, awesome life. To balance what we know and how we feel is the idyllic fantasy of the intellectual. And while some perfect balance of emotional cognition and intellectual fact-taking may never be possible, behaving in such a way that emulates a desire for that balance is very much so.

Chapter Nine

End the Culture, End the War

To conclude part III and to make my final case, I wish to explore the most important question of this book: how do we redress the excesses of the culture wars as a kind of political discourse? The culture wars as a discourse create an advanced echo chamber, the likes of which has never been seen before, through a personalization of certain artifacts which represent a particular feeling we have about ourselves as individuals and as members of the groups we associate with. Furthermore, they create an environment of violence and oppression, where the freedom and mere existence of others must be reduced and annihilated. They are what they say they are. A war. But this war is a vitriolic and unnecessarily brutal one when its content is confined to the imagination of its warriors. The material political impacts on American society, and society net large, have been detrimental. Democratic freedoms and institutions are reduced to rubble out of fear that the "bad guys" will get them. People trust each other less and less over ideas each have about the other that are, more often than they are not, made up or exaggerated. And an acceptance of violence and abuse rises as rather than being forced to reconcile with one another and the world, we choose to simply blow it all up if we can't be told everything we think and do is unequivocally true and wholly good.

My solution, after studying these culture wars as a discourse for the better part of a year and a half, is simple:

If one truly wishes to avoid these excesses of the culture wars, one must abstract themself from culture altogether.

We have determined, for one, that this thing called "culture" is far more than what music you like, what food you eat or what clothes you wear. Culture is both a social and political force. Culture is a collection of physical artifacts and memories that combine to produce a certain feeling about a collective of people. This collective of people, with their artifacts and their histories, in turn, produces us. But to ideologically abstract oneself from this context seems not merely impossible, but also as a form of ideological suicide. For one, let's not pretend what is true. It is the case that we come from particular experiences created by the social circles which raise and form around us. These circles and their ways of life are carried down through means of memories of the past and artifacts which prove its existence, and tell us what those people who have come and since gone did, and if they were explicit enough, what we ought to be doing as well. More than just being the result of this force, we also draw a distinct *value* from it. Our cultures inspire in us confidence, camaraderie with others, independence and respect for our elders. They teach us to be our authentic selves, to carry on the ideals of those who came before us, and to never back down from those who may threaten us because of the kind of person it has made us. They teach us to contribute to our communities, to help each other out, and to practice grace with others. Among the many plethora of values produced by the world's belief systems, social or political, they all inspire different feelings of self and society that can contribute to the collective project of living simultaneously in productive ways.

And pluralistic societies reflect this notion that all the values these diverse systems create cannot merely coexist, but can also contribute to a larger idea of existence that transcends them all with respect to their origin. It has produced the modern democracy as we conceive it, a passion project of our ancestors from across the globe all gathered together, fighting for an establishment and maintenance of collective society that, to this day, we still mend ever closer to what we feel like a diverse and free society ought to look and behave like. Ideally, it accepts and promotes a multiplicity of these values simultaneously: Independence *and* community. Caring for ourselves *and* for others. Self-reliance *and* social welfare. Competence *and* likability. Unchanging facts *and* emotional cognition. And the goal of this society may be espoused to form a "perfect" balance of all these values. But the truth is we all know such perfection is unattainable. Perhaps the only useful delusion in the history of man, we speak into existence an idea that such perfect balance is possible, so that we may feel motivated to achieve it. This society takes the different ways of life, and it does not pit them against each other in a battlefield or a boxing ring or a marketplace of ideas to determine who will "win" against the other.

This notion is absurd. Rather, it condemns them to perhaps the greatest punishment to the deluded ideologue: merely existing with others. And for its maintenance, it takes from them those values which will make it stronger, faster, better suited to meet the challenges of existing alongside all the various societies which outline the earth.

This society does not merely cherry pick "the good parts" of the ideologies of its inhabitants and discard "the bad parts." The definitional value and functional infrastructure needed to accomplish that goal would be an insurmountable task to accomplish. As well, this society does not delude itself into assuming perfect harmony will occur vis a vis the integration of an ideologically diverse society. Culture wars are an inevitable feature of living a certain way, knowing certain things, and coming into contact with other ways of being and the facts which deviate from our perfect truths. The real challenge of the pluralistic society is rather how it facilitates that conflict. This constitutes the rule of law. An institutional structure formed from the collective agreement of its society, the pluralistic society derives an elastic system of rules and procedures which denote what it accepts, what it rejects, and what lies in between, and how to address when the individual breaks the agreement made by society. The folly of modern society, and the delusion of ideology, is that such work will ever be done. That there is some perfect truth being worked towards which, once achieved, will accomplish the task of constructing the perfect society. We have already established this is absurd. The belief in perfect good and its absolute attainment is nothing short of delusion and hysteria. Rather, the pluralistic society keeps its laws elastic so that none may ever crystalize themselves to the foundation of society only to be found out for being reductionist, incomplete, or plainly out of date and incongruent with society.

What does this mean of the rule of law, then? What of constitutions which are meant to protect the basis of *all* legal philosophies and laws therein? Once again, the delusion of a perfect society proves useful, even in the recognition of its nature as a delusion. The establishment of a priori natural rights which are unchanging and all-encompassing is, truthfully, nothing short of just another feeling we have about ourselves and the world. Their permanence is only precedented by whether or not we acknowledge it, and it is in fact the great work of civil rights activists and human rights institutions around the world which must tirelessly work to *make* these rights, which too the pluralistic society must agree upon and refine to their understanding of self and society, permanent in nature. This does not mean merely throwing out these universals is an acceptable behavior, even if it is an acceptable thought. What it does mean, however, is that we cannot establish them in permanence arbitrarily and simply assume they will withstand the test of time, as the delusions of ideology will receive them as being situationally invalid for their political opposition, slowly stripping them until their permanence is lost in the shadows of totalitarianism.

And it is this totalitarianism that represents the threat of rejecting the pluralistic society in favor of the perfect truth of one's culture as a political and social force. The discourse of the culture wars reveals to us the uglier parts of ourselves as we reject democracy, each other and the world if it does not conform to our myths and fantasies about it. Even amidst all the wonderful things our cultures do, what they do to inform our character, our beliefs, and our attitudes towards other people. This commitment to it, as it provides us with an understanding of who we are, of who others are, and of how the world does and ought to work, can become too much. There is a point where camaraderie turns into a demand for extreme, unquestioning loyalty. It invents a delusion of "one truth" which takes the material world in which we live and its facts, and binds it together with our emotional cognitions of it into an amalgamation of facts and feelings that is supposed to represent all of reality in a single foul swoop. This aesthetic "truth" hypocritically speaks of facts and objective reality, rejecting the notion of discursive reinvention, yet engages in it wholesale. Worse yet, this inception of "truth" creates a necessity for the reinforcement of itself and obedience towards it. The illusory merger of moral feelings and information creates an idea which says that such "truth" is a force for good, and must be treated with such an unwavering respect and reverence that to deviate from it, even if merely on the basis of applicability or factuality, is an act of treason. To fight against it? You become an existential threat to the totalitarian ideologue.

The invention of the evil other further reinforces the illusion of "one truth" and the moral value of good assigned to it by dichotomizing it with an antithetical force of moral evil. This character, in the melodramatic prose of the culture warrior who has committed themselves wholly to their righteous truth, serves two primary functions. First, their description as being the product of pure evil opposed to our pure good is meant to explain the reason those who deviate from the perfect truth do so. It intentionally delegitimizes the experiences of other people, and the beliefs they draw from them. We recognize how culture creates us. But the culture wars cause us to engage in what psychology calls the fundamental attribution error, wherein we assume that the actions of other people are simply the result of the "kind" of person they are, negating the possibility they are the result of their own environments and experiences.[192] It specifically does this in the context of framing one's own behaviors as being the result of our environments, of the experiences that create us. This error attempts to assign agency to the evil other as being intentional and devoid of context. It simultaneously flushes out context for our behaviors, creating an aesthetic of lack of agency around us. Our goodness is informed by reasons, by experiences and beliefs we form from this, rightly so. The evil other has no such experiences. They have no reason to oppose us but out of pure hatred, pure evil.

Furthermore, this aesthetic reconstruction of our conflict with others accomplishes the self-victimization inherent to culture wars discourse. Because we are the result of our environments and experiences, we are helpless to the events which happen to us, which drive our behavior. Our attacks

---

[192] Mcleod, "Fundamental Attribution Error Theory in Psychology," para. 1.

against the evil other are necessitated by the experiences we have had with them as they needlessly antagonize us. They, on the other hand, have no reason to antagonize us. We have done nothing to provoke them because our experiences are real, and the values we derive from them are pure. Which brings us to the second function of the evil other as a moral type in the culture wars. In contextualizing others as pure evil, devoid of experiential or environmental contributing factors to their behaviors or beliefs, we justify retaliation of an increasingly violent nature. Their evil cannot be reasoned with. It cannot be cured or reversed. The evil other is simply evil, and their rejection from civil society or utter annihilation are the only way to prevent or reduce their harm to society, or potentiality thereof. Every action taken by others in defense against our righteous battle against them can be reconstructed into another reason why the other is both pure evil and unrelentingly antagonistic against us. With no reason to explain their retaliation, which in reality is the mirror image of ours, increasing our acceptance of violent acts to force out the pure evil they endorse is part of the culture warrior's reconstruction of reality when in conflict with others.

The society of the culture warrior, the outcome of their domination of the evil other, is a totalitarian nanny state which perpetually inspects for and enforces the purity and moral truth of their obscured reality. Political ideologies attempt to reject the notion that force will be required to attain this society. Given the obvious nature of their universal truth, it will simply become realized by the masses, and accepted willingly. This, too, is part of the delusion of the culture warrior, incorporating resistance against their perfect truth into their reconstruction of the world. Resistance to an enforced "truth" becomes part of a larger conspiracy of lies. The evil lie rejects the good truth because it is evil, and its influence has "got" a hold on average citizens, who become victims much like we do to the evil other. Force employed against these people is not a senseless act of political violence, but instead becomes a necessary measure to stomp out the evil lie. Propaganda becomes not an exaggeration or total falsification campaign by an aggressive government, but a pivotal truth-sharing campaign to prevent the spread of the evil other's false reality in the collective society. The development of the culture warrior's view of the world, in the context of the dichotomous battle between an absolute good and an abject evil which they are always at the center of, leads to a development in anti-democratic, totalitarian political views, an acceptance of violence as a mediator for disagreement, and a delusion in which all things combine to create a single unit of "truth" that aligns with their moral-emotional cognition of life and the world.

The solution to abstract from culture altogether seems to be a jarring antithetical to falling into the pits of delusion. But its opposition misses a critical part of ideological abstraction that I think is what makes it such an unappealing strategy to them. One assumes, in the same light as the warped discourse of the culture wars has them think of their conflicts, that the choice between the delusion of ideology and the abstraction from it is a dichotomous absolute. That one must either wholly embrace the mythification of the world presented by only accepting a specific series of experiences as legitimate and its moralities therein, or one must wholly reject such mythification, and fling oneself into the darkness of the moral void. This is not the case. One *is* capable of being both made from the culture which produced them, drawing from it their character and beliefs, *and* able to abstract themselves from it in order to understand the limitations of their culture and how its war with others is the result of a partial reconstruction of reality not being wholly accurate or good.

All of the credentials we gave culture as a social and political force remain intact even in the instance of abstraction. The assumption of a dichotomous rejection of what culture makes of us in our attempt to see it from outside itself are absurd and reductionist. They attempt to reframe culture as a dominating force which orders us around, telling us what and who we ought to be. But this view does not understand how it is that culture creates people. The invention of culture, its artifacts and history, into the culmination of people and collectives, is not a sign of the enduring supremacy of a particular way of life. This is a misconception on the part of humanity. Our cultures persist, not because they are destined to rule the world or command existence in any particular way. Their persistence is a sign of the love we have for those who came before us, products and producers of our culture the same as we are. Our commitment to what they tell us we ought to be like, even in the instance in which it is misguided or deluded, is out of a shared understanding of the world, and a perceived value in that understanding. The artifacts it produces are the outcomes of people bonding over their shared experiences, shared beliefs, and the ongoing sharing of ideas. Their lasting significance is indicative of not merely our passion for ourselves, but the passion for those who come after us for what we were and what we created. They look at us, much as we looked up at our ancestors, with a sense of guidance and admiration. This sensible feeling we wish to accomplish in the construction and commitment to a way of life, a society, is shared by those who come after us, treading through similar experiences as ours.

All the same, to be abstracted from our culture is to understand the limitations of culture in that it is the outcome of a series of experiences in particular environments, at a particular point in time, received in a particular way. The human experience of consciousness is universal, but the different results of that experience vary so minutely person-to-person that even within the same "side," a shared feeling about the world informed by a shared experience of it is bound to carry an underlying complexity of circumstantial nuances. We merely gloss over these nuances in search of the shared feeling we see in others. This is not inherently bad, the abstracted culture warrior will find. But it does lead to an acceptance of the self, of experience, and of social and political goals and realities that are two dimensional and reductive. The abstracted culture warrior will recognize that others, most especially others who do not share our feelings or experiences or knowledge at all, still came to their way of being as we did. Through the experience of consciousness and the subsequent development of self it produced, within the context of a social paradigm constructed by those with whom they were born and live with. Through words and political actions, we all are shaped, and can shape.

The "truth" of reality that supersedes all the various "realities" of partisans and diverse cultures isn't some conspiracy that is being kept from the people. It isn't a moral lesson that, if only people would see past their selfish biases, they would finally be "awake" to the truth of the world. In fact, the "truth" of our world is quite boring. It is a collection of material truths, of objective, measurable, replicable and testable things which do happen and can happen, within a degree of probability. But this set of truths is enhanced through the experience of consciousness, as meaning is derived from and applied to these material realities in a sensible feeling of the world. In a collective society, how we achieve this "truth" comes from when we reconcile our feelings, morals and character with both the material facts that may defy them, and more importantly with each other. We must be able to approach one another with an acknowledgement of the futility, imperfection and emotional precedence of our views of the world, and the reason we designed them. The abstracted culture warrior can do this, as it actually makes them a better arguer of their own positions. To see this difference between the unified "truth" of the culture wars and their need to be enforced, and the intertwined realities of a species which infinitely interprets a series of material facts, is to be able to see in others what one can humbly see in themself: fallibility.

The act of reconciliation is not inherently easy. To look at oneself and the environment which created one, and to admit its fallibility feels like an existential threat. But the idea that who we are and what we believe within the complex of our cultures must be a universal absolute in order to be functional is wrong, and a byproduct of poor use of our brain evolution. We don't have to cling to certainties and abject moralities in order to be effective members of society, have strong social networks with interesting and diverse people, or to see in ourselves a goodness that radiates in the world we live in. This myth is the greatest of them all. The pluralistic collective is capable of bringing together people who bond strongly, not over the shared feelings or experiences that make them, but over their shared pursuit of a better society which does not constitute itself on the lie of a universal absolute. Referring back to the American Constitution, the "more perfect union" is not more perfect in that it is more aligned around some perfect truth under the banner of a particular political and social movement. The pursuit of a more perfect union is the mere act of politics, the mere act of a shared collective which transcends the motivations of any one particular way of life, but recognizes the work of cultures which cross over into one another, creating broader cultural schemas which will produce future generations or causing conflict. The act of politics, forever ongoing, is the materialization of ideological reconciliation. The designing of shared systems of government give a multiplicity a political union under which it can function both independently of other cultures and in a delicate dance alongside them. The establishment of shared customs, moralities and laws lays the groundwork for what a collective society will accept within its political union and how it will redress those who defy this collective agreement, intentionally or by accident. And a shared space in which society integrates itself, in defiance of ideological segregation, forces us to inhabit spaces with one another, forces us to interact with one another, and forces us, over time, to form unions with one another in the form of our social groups, political institutions, and personal relationships.

It should also never be expected to eventually produce some final product of ultimate freedom or unity. This remains the delusion of the culture wars. Instead, to abstract is to recognize both where we come from separate from one another, and the collective bonds we form when we realize we have no choice but to live amongst one another. This does not require us to give up our principles and the experiences that constitute them. But it does require us to sit in a pool of self reflection at all times. Much as we ought to question all that we are provided with by external forces, we ought to as well question ourselves, our own biases, our own motivations, our own ways of being. For it is not only the other who may lie or manipulate you into behaving a certain way, but it is also yourself who will do so. In this relationship with ourselves and with others, I believe we avoid the excesses of the culture wars, in remaining firmly in acknowledgement of what created us and how it produces in us the feeling of who we are, and how that feeling is inspired all the same in everyone else.

This reconciliation between the cultural schemas that constitute us and our feelings of self-and-society will not negate all ways of life as arbitrary and defenseless. Society need not collapse into utter chaos at the recognition that we fight for a sensible feeling of society instead of a universal truth that ought to be enforced. Rather, the reconciliation of ideology—with itself and with others—will imbue us and our lives with meaning. We will know that culture is so much more than an abject good whose totalitarian rule will maximize the flourishing of a pure and noble society, but that it is a sense of self that binds people together through experience and interpretation. Moreso, this force called "culture," both socially and politically, acts in this way for everyone. In reconciling that, we too gain a more human view of the evil other. Their evil is trivialized into our own fear. And if we have the resolve and the courage to do so, reconciling our culture wars will lead us to a point at which we can reach out into the darkness to find these others, where together we can march a new path under the light of a shared torch.

Conclusion

What are the culture wars? Are they a set of issues? Is their primary concern religion, or gender, or political freedoms? We have explored this question and its implications throughout *The Culture Bores*, and I think we have found out the culture wars go beyond any set of issues, especially past the "earlier culture war really ... about secularization, and positions were tied to theologies and justified on the basis of theologies,"[193] that James Davison Hunter saw in the 90s. Instead, they have evolved into a kind of politics all their own, consumed with notions of morality and political outcomes that will reflect and reinforce this morality which binds itself to the idea of truth.

The discourse of culture wars approaches any political or social issue and feels a deep sense of emotion about it, drawing from the illusory moral truth designed from one's life experiences as being indicative of both how the world *is* and how it *ought to* be. Furthermore, it uses divisive and passionate rhetoric to reinforce this idea of moral and factual unity in a single object of "truth" which is uncompromising, aesthetically complete, and incorruptible. The discourse of culture wars discursively reconstruct events and political stimuli within the framework of its moral absolution both to reinforce its moral typology as well as to create a

---

[193] Stanton, "How the 'Culture War' Could Break Democracy," para. 6.

rhetorical outline that will be presented to audiences in a particular spectacle of emotional gravity, aesthetic totality and shocking violence. On this note, the culture wars also, in an ever-escalating last resort, build the foundation for an environment which accepts violence as an acceptable political act in the face of retribution from others and potential failure to "win" these wars by means of discursive subjugation.

But this does not mean the culture wars are an inevitable development in politics. We closed our previous chapter exploring the ability to constitute political realities that are no less passionate and volatile than they are now. Let's not be mistaken, to have a view of the world is not inherently wrong, even if it contradicts the views of others. If anything, we have thoroughly established an understanding of human identity and its development that helps us understand why it is that people are who they are and do what they do in the context of their lives. However, what we do argue is that the culture wars as a way of doing politics is unstable, prone to anti-democratic and violent tactics and justifications, and ultimately oppressive. The culture wars are imagined battles constituted by the feelings of its warriors and their understanding of our shared reality. And it is only right that they argue over their feelings of how the world ought to be based on what they know, and how they've lived. But to foster a political discourse that questions the value of democracy, of the freedoms it provides as an institution, and accepts violence to force through this way of being in defiance of the shared agreements of our collectives is dangerous to the well being of modern society. As Hunter recognized, "Democracy, in my view, is an agreement that we will not kill each other over our differences, but instead we'll talk through those differences. And part of what's troubling is that I'm beginning to see signs of the justification for violence on both sides."[194]

The culture wars is a dangerous kind of politics which callously disregards the institution of democracy as counterintuitive to its perfect moral truth. But while its truth does much to create in us a feeling of self, a feeling of efficacy in politics and in our communities, and a feeling of goodness in who we are, the reality is all of these things require serious and constant self reflection. They are not inherent qualities reflected by a particular way of life. Collective societies espouse this value, and the work of politics is to constantly fashion the environments in which this self reflection can occur. Furthermore, pluralistic collectives take that value one step further, creating an environment in which a multiplicity of "selves" must reconcile with one another who they are as individuals, who they are as groups, and who they are as a totality.

We close our argument with the acknowledgement that this work is never done, and that while unsatisfying, the sense of argument that defines our politics is actually a sign that it is working. To achieve a status of abject peace, where all political differences are resolved, and society stands completely in unison on every issue that once plagued us, is a sign of totalitarianism. Democracy forces us to reconcile both how we feel about ourselves and how

---

[194] Stanton, para. 32.

we feel about the world with both the material information that constitutes the world and the feelings of others about it. Unlike the culture wars, it allows us to contend for our way of life without slipping into the pits of delusion and engaging violence against everyone outside. And while it may never resolve the contention between political groups, it may be, in fact, such contention that stands tall and proud as proof of our freedom.

Bibliography

Alfonseca, Kiara. "Culture Wars: How Identity Became the Center of Politics in America." ABC News, July 7, 2023. https://abcnews.go.com/US/culture-wars-identity-center-politics-america/story?id=100768380.

Alliance Defending Freedom. "Masterpiece Cakeshop v. Colorado Civil Rights Commission." Alliance Defending Freedom, June 4, 2018. https://adflegal.org/case/masterpiece-cakeshop-v-colorado-civil-rights-commission.

American Civil Liberties Union. "Masterpiece Cakeshop v. Colorado Civil Rights Commission - FAQ," June 8, 2018. https://www.aclu.org/documents/masterpiece-cakeshop-v-colorado-civil-rights-commission-faq.

American Oversight. "The Trump Administration's Transgender Military Ban," July 15, 2024. https://www.americanoversight.org/investigation/trump-administrations-transgender-military-ban.

Anker, Elisabeth R. *Orgies of Feeling: Melodrama and the Politics of Freedom.* Durham, NC: Duke University Press, 2014.

Anthony, Andrew. "Everything You Wanted to Know about the Culture Wars – but Were Afraid to Ask." *The Guardian*, June 13, 2021, sec. World news. https://www.theguardian.com/world/2021/jun/13/everything-you-wanted-to-know-about-the-culture-wars-but-were-afraid-to-ask.

Baele, Stephane J., Katharine Boyd, Travis G. Coan, and Elahe Naserian. "Lethal Words: An Integrated Model of Violent Extremists' Language." *Studies in Conflict & Terrorism* 0, no. 0 (May 2023): 1–26. https://doi.org/10.1080/1057610X.2023.2213963.

Banks, Jim. "Lean Into Culture War | Republican Study Committee," April 26, 2022. http://rsc-hern.house.gov/lean-culture-war.

Barnes, Katie. "Transgender Athletes and the Laws That Govern Participation." ESPN.com, August 24, 2023. https://www.espn.com/espn/story/_/id/38209262/transgender-athlete-laws-state-legislation-science.

BBC. "Danger of Mutually Assured Destruction -

Managing the Cold War 1962-85 - Higher History Revision," May 1, 2024. https://www.bbc.co.uk/bitesize/guides/z9jpn39/revision/2.

Beard, Mary. *SPQR: A History of Ancient Rome.* London: Profile Books, 2015.

Biesecker, Michael, Alanna D. Richer, Jim Mustian, and Michael Balsamo. "Trump Assassination Attempt: What We Know about the Suspect | AP News." News site. AP News, July 15, 2024. https://apnews.com/article/trump-assassination-attempt-thomas-matthew-crooks-shooter-881581c46c07025898027143fc9132e5.

Binkley, Collin. "'Too Hyperbolic'? School Board Parental Rights Push Falters." AP News, November 14, 2022. https://apnews.com/article/school-boards-politics-parents-rights-2bed4680bdedd4c866e046136630a9e8.

BOOM: Shapiro SETTLES Culture War ORIGINS Debate, 2021. https://www.youtube.com/watch?v=udgtS1FO6oM.

Buchanan, Patrick J. "1992 Republican National Convention Speech." *Patrick J. Buchanan - Official Website* (blog), August 17, 1992.

https://buchanan.org/blog/1992-republican-national-convention-speech-148.

Campbell, Angus, Philip E. Converse, Warren E. Miller, and Donald E. Stokes. *The American Voter*. Chicago, IL: University of Chicago Press, 1960. https://press.uchicago.edu/ucp/books/book/chicago/A/bo24047989.html.

Chemerinsky, Erwin. "Not a Masterpiece: The Supreme Court's Decision in Masterpiece Cakeshop v. Colorado Civil Rights Commission." American Bar Association, February 6, 2024. https://www.americanbar.org/groups/crsj/publications/human_rights_magazine_home/the-ongoing-challenge-to-define-free-speech/not-a-masterpiece/.

Clark, Cory J., Brittany S. Liu, Bo M. Winegard, and Peter H. Ditto. "Tribalism Is Human Nature." *Current Directions in Psychological Science* 28, no. 6 (December 1, 2019): 587–92. https://doi.org/10.1177/0963721419862289.

CNN. "Biden-Trump Debate Transcript | CNN Politics," June 28, 2024. https://www.cnn.com/2024/06/27/politics/read-biden-trump-debate-rush-transcript/ind

ex.html.

Coach, 2022.
https://www.youtube.com/watch?v=h7iHpn
C7hmU.

Colarossi, Natalie. "California School Board
Members Caught on Tape Mocking Parents
Upset About School Closures." Newsweek,
February 19, 2021.
https://www.newsweek.com/san-francisco-sc
hool-board-members-caught-tape-mocking-p
arents-upset-about-school-closures-1570565.

Colvin, Jill, Julie Carr Smyth, Coleen Long, Eric
Tucker, Michael Balsamo, and Michel L.
Price. "Trump Survives Apparent
Assassination Attempt, One Attendee Killed,
FBI Investigates | AP News." News site. AP
News, July 14, 2024.
https://apnews.com/article/trump-vp-vance-
rubio-7c7ba6b99b5f38d2d840ed95b2fdc3e5.

Conlan, Timothy J. "The Changing Politics of
American Federalism." *State & Local
Government Review* 49, no. 3 (2017):
170–83.

Creanza, Nicole, Oren Kolodny, and Marcus W.
Feldman. "Cultural Evolutionary Theory:
How Culture Evolves and Why It Matters."
Proceedings of the National Academy of

Sciences 114, no. 30 (July 25, 2017): 7782–89. https://doi.org/10.1073/pnas.1620732114.

"DEI Must DIE!" - Charlie Kirk Goes off Against the DEI Movement, 2023. https://www.youtube.com/watch?v=3ZU1h6urZxo.

Drum, Kevin. "If You Hate the Culture Wars, Blame Liberals." *Kevin Drum* (blog), July 3, 2021. https://jabberwocking.com/if-you-hate-the-culture-wars-blame-liberals/.

Emery, David. "A History of the 'War on Christmas.'" Snopes, November 29, 2017. https://www.snopes.com/news/2017/11/29/the-war-on-christmas/.

Finkel, Eli J., Christopher A. Bail, Mina Cikara, Peter H. Ditto, Shanto Iyengar, Samara Klar, Lilliana Mason, et al. "Political Sectarianism in America." *Science* 370, no. 6516 (October 30, 2020): 533–36. https://doi.org/10.1126/science.abe1715.

Gaffney, Theresa. "Physicians Say Transgender Sports Bans Are a Health Issue." *STAT* (blog), September 19, 2023. https://www.statnews.com/2023/09/19/transgender-sports-debate-consider-health-of-trans-youth/.

Garland, Merrick. "Office of Public Affairs |
Justice Department Addresses Violent
Threats Against School Officials and Teachers
| United States Department of Justice."
doj.gov, October 4, 2021.
https://www.justice.gov/opa/pr/justice-depa
rtment-addresses-violent-threats-against-sch
ool-officials-and-teachers.

Goldman, Alan H. "The Broad View of Aesthetic
Experience." *The Journal of Aesthetics and
Art Criticism* 71, no. 4 (2013): 323–33.

"Governor DeSantis Announces Legislative
Proposal to Stop W.O.K.E. Activism and
Critical Race Theory in Schools and
Corporations," December 24, 2022.
https://www.flgov.com/2021/12/15/governor
-desantis-announces-legislative-proposal-to-s
top-w-o-k-e-activism-and-critical-race-theory
-in-schools-and-corporations/.

"Governor Ron DeSantis Highlights
Administration's Major Accomplishments of
2020," December 24, 2022.
https://www.flgov.com/2020/12/22/governo
r-ron-desantis-highlights-administrations-ma
jor-accomplishments-of-2020/.

Gracia, Gabriel Borelli and Shanay. "What
Americans Know about Their Government."

Pew Research Center (blog), November 7, 2023. https://www.pewresearch.org/short-reads/2023/11/07/what-americans-know-about-their-government/.

Graham, Matthew H., and Milan W. Svolik. "Democracy in America? Partisanship, Polarization, and the Robustness of Support for Democracy in the United States." *American Political Science Review* 114, no. 2 (May 2020): 392–409. https://doi.org/10.1017/S0003055420000052.

Haidt, Jonathan. *The Righteous Mind: Why Good People Are Divided by Politics and Religion.* The Righteous Mind: Why Good People Are Divided by Politics and Religion. New York, NY, US: Pantheon/Random House, 2012.

Hamedy, Saba. "Did Trump Stop the 'War on Christmas'? Some Say Yes | CNN Politics." News site. CNN, December 22, 2017. https://www.cnn.com/2017/12/22/politics/donald-trump-war-on-christmas/index.html.

Hare, Brian. "Survival of the Friendliest: Homo Sapiens Evolved via Selection for Prosociality." *Annual Review of Psychology* 68, no. 1 (2017): 155–86.

https://doi.org/10.1146/annurev-psych-0104
16-044201.

Hoffe, O. "Pluralism and Toleration." In
*International Encyclopedia of the Social &
Behavioral Sciences*, edited by Neil J.
Smelser and Paul B. Baltes, 11520–26.
Oxford: Pergamon, 2001.
https://doi.org/10.1016/B0-08-043076-7/01
064-0.

Hofstadter, Richard. "The Paranoid Style in
American Politics." Harper's Magazine,
November 1964.
https://harpers.org/archive/1964/11/the-par
anoid-style-in-american-politics/.

———. "The Paranoid Style in American Politics."
Harper's Magazine, November 1964.
https://harpers.org/archive/1964/11/the-par
anoid-style-in-american-politics/.

Hogg, Michael A. "Social Identity Theory." In
*Understanding Peace and Conflict Through
Social Identity Theory: Contemporary
Global Perspectives*, edited by Shelley
McKeown, Reeshma Haji, and Neil Ferguson,
3–17. Peace Psychology Book Series. Cham:
Springer International Publishing, 2016.
https://doi.org/10.1007/978-3-319-29869-6
_1.

Homer-Dixon, Thomas, Jonathan Leader
    Maynard, Matto Mildenberger, Manjana
    Milkoreit, Steven J. Mock, Stephen Quilley,
    Tobias Schröder, and Paul Thagard. "A
    Complex Systems Approach to the Study of
    Ideology: Cognitive-Affective Structures and
    the Dynamics of Belief Systems." *Journal of
    Social and Political Psychology* 1, no. 1
    (December 16, 2013): 337–63.
    https://doi.org/10.5964/jspp.v1i1.36.

Human Rights Campaign. "Get the Facts about
    Transgender & Non-Binary Athletes,"
    February 23, 2024.
    https://www.hrc.org/resources/get-the-facts-
    about-transgender-non-binary-athletes.

Ilievski, Nikola Lj. "THE CONCEPT OF
    POLITICAL INTEGRATION: THE
    PERSPECTIVES OF NEOFUNCTIONALIST
    THEORY." *Journal of Liberty and
    International Affairs* 1, no. 1 (2015).
    https://www.e-jlia.com/index.php/jlia/articl
    e/view/13.

*I'm Running to Reverse the Decline of Our
    Nation*, 2023.
    https://www.youtube.com/watch?v=FJI4z-N
    QPGk.

Jay, Martin. "'The Aesthetic Ideology' as Ideology;

Or, What Does It Mean to Aestheticize Politics?" *Cultural Critique*, no. 21 (1992): 41–61. https://doi.org/10.2307/1354116.

Jensen, Keith, Amrisha Vaish, and Marco F. H. Schmidt. "The Emergence of Human Prosociality: Aligning with Others through Feelings, Concerns, and Norms." *Frontiers in Psychology* 5 (2014). https://www.frontiersin.org/articles/10.3389/fpsyg.2014.00822.

Joe Biden Launches His Campaign For President: Let's Finish the Job, 2023. https://www.youtube.com/watch?v=ChjibtXoUzU.

Jones, Jeffrey M. "More Say Birth Gender Should Dictate Sports Participation." Gallup.com, June 12, 2023. https://news.gallup.com/poll/507023/say-birth-gender-dictate-sports-participation.aspx.

Kingkade, Tyler, and Marissa Parra. "OK Schools Head Vows Sanctions for Teachers Who Won't Teach the Bible." NBC News, June 28, 2024. https://www.nbcnews.com/news/oklahoma-schools-bible-ryan-walters-teachers-license-rcna159548.

Kohn, Margaret, and Kavita Reddy.

"Colonialism." In *The Stanford Encyclopedia of Philosophy*, edited by Edward N. Zalta and Uri Nodelman, Spring 2023. Metaphysics Research Lab, Stanford University, 2023. https://plato.stanford.edu/archives/spr2023/entries/colonialism/.

Laukaitis, John J. "The Academy on the Firing Line." *American Educational History Journal* 40, no. 1/2 (March 2013): 129–40.

Levenson, Eric. "How an Ivy League Swimmer Became the Face of the Debate on Transgender Women in Sports." CNN, February 22, 2022. https://www.cnn.com/2022/02/22/us/lia-thomas-transgender-swimmer-ivy-league/index.html.

Lonas, Lexi. "How School Boards Became One of Democracy's Front Lines." Text. *The Hill* (blog), November 26, 2023. https://thehill.com/homenews/education/4323139-american-school-boards/.

Loudoun County School Board BLASTED Over Bombshell Daily Wire Exposé, 2021. https://www.youtube.com/watch?v=1uyNtbNzJ1o.

Mariani, John. "How Immigrants From Everywhere Made American Food The Most

Diverse In The World." Forbes, July 9, 2023. https://www.forbes.com/sites/johnmariani/2020/04/13/how-immigrants-from-everywhere-made-american-food-the-most-diverse-in-the-world/.

Martin, James. "Rhetoric, Discourse and the Hermeneutics of Public Speech," 2022. https://doi.org/10.1177/0263395720933779.

Masterpiece Cakeshop. "Wedding | MASTERPIECE CAKESHOP," February 21, 2024. https://masterpiececakes.com/wedding-cakes/.

Mcleod, Paul. "Fundamental Attribution Error Theory in Psychology." Simply Psychology, June 15, 2023. https://www.simplypsychology.org/fundamental-attribution.html.

Menand, Louis. "How Cultural Anthropologists Redefined Humanity." *The New Yorker*, August 19, 2019. https://www.newyorker.com/magazine/2019/08/26/how-cultural-anthropologists-redefined-humanity.

Migdon, Brooke. "Haley Calls Transgender Athletes in Sports 'the Women's Issue of Our Time.'" Text. *The Hill* (blog), June 5, 2023.

https://thehill.com/homenews/campaign/40
34876-haley-calls-transgender-athletes-in-sp
orts-the-womens-issue-of-our-time/.

Miles, Andrew, and Stephen Vaisey. "Morality and
Politics: Comparing Alternate Theories."
Social Science Research 53 (September 1,
2015): 252–69.
https://doi.org/10.1016/j.ssresearch.2015.06.
002.

Mill, John Stuart. *On Liberty*. Kitchener, Ont.:
Batoche Books, 2001.

Nielsen, Henrik Kaare. "Totalizing Aesthetics?
Aesthetic Theory and the Aestheticization of
Everyday Life." *The Nordic Journal of
Aesthetics* 17, no. 32 (2005).
https://doi.org/10.7146/nja.v17i32.2976.

O'Brien, Falyn. "The Lugar Center and McCourt
School Release Latest Bipartisan Index
Rankings for Congress." *McCourt School of
Public Policy* (blog), May 14, 2024.
https://mccourt.georgetown.edu/news/bipar
tisan-index-2023-118th-congress/.

Ollstein, Alice Miranda. "Trump Administration
Issues Rule to Strip Millions from Planned
Parenthood." POLITICO, February 22, 2019.
https://www.politico.com/story/2019/02/22
/planned-parenthood-funding-trump-116403

8.

PBS NewsHour. "How 'the War on Christmas' Became a Political Rallying Cry," December 25, 2017. https://www.pbs.org/newshour/show/how-the-war-on-christmas-became-a-political-rallying-cry.

Pew Research Center - U.S. Politics & Policy. "4. The Republican and Democratic Parties," September 19, 2023. https://www.pewresearch.org/politics/2023/09/19/the-republican-and-democratic-parties/.

Prestwick House. "Understanding the New Florida B.E.S.T. Standards," December 24, 2022. https://www.prestwickhouse.com/blog/post/2020/07/understanding-the-new-florida-best-standards.

Rancière, Jacques. "The Aesthetic Dimension: Aesthetics, Politics, Knowledge." *Critical Inquiry* 36, no. 1 (2009): 1–19. https://doi.org/10.1086/606120.

Rao, Ashwin, Siyi Guo, Sze-Yuh Nina Wang, Fred Morstatter, and Kristina Lerman. "Pandemic Culture Wars: Partisan Asymmetries in the Moral Language of COVID-19 Discussions."

arXiv, May 29, 2023.
https://doi.org/10.48550/arXiv.2305.18533.

Reed, Brad. "'Fox & Friends' Segment Makes Dubious Claim That 'Radicals' Are Waging a War on Christmas." Salon, December 16, 2019.
https://www.salon.com/2019/12/16/fox-frie nds-segment-makes-dubious-claim-that-radi cals-are-waging-a-war-on-christmas_partner /.

Riner, Robin Conley. "Language and Violence." *Oxford Research Encyclopedia of Anthropology*, December 13, 2023.
https://oxfordre.com/anthropology/display/ 10.1093/acrefore/9780190854584.001.0001/ acrefore-9780190854584-e-620.

"Rock and Roll | History, Songs, Artists, & Facts | Britannica," June 7, 2023.
https://www.britannica.com/art/rock-and-ro ll-early-style-of-rock-music.

Rogers, W. Hayward. "Some Methodological Difficulties in Anthony Downs's An Economic Theory of Democracy." *The American Political Science Review* 53, no. 2 (1959): 483–85. https://doi.org/10.2307/1952158.

Salvanto, Anthony, Jennifer De Pinto, and Fred Backus. "Should the next House Speaker

Work across the Aisle? Be Loyal to Trump? -
CBS News," October 8, 2023.
https://www.cbsnews.com/news/should-the-
next-house-speaker-work-across-the-aisle-be
-loyal-to-trump/.

Santoso, Lie Philip, Randolph T. Stevenson, and
Simon Weschle. "What Drives Perceptions of
Partisan Cooperation?" *Political Science
Research and Methods*, June 19, 2023, 1–9.
https://doi.org/10.1017/psrm.2023.20.

Schattschneider, E.E. "The Contagiousness of
Conflict." In *The Semisovereign People*, 1–19.
Holt, Rineheart and Winston, 1960.

*School Boards Become Battlegrounds for
Nation's Divisions on Race, Gender and
More*, 2023.
https://www.youtube.com/watch?v=JtTfK6s
mb4c.

*SCOTUS Same-Sex Wedding Cake Decision: How
Both Sides Say They Got Here Today*, 2018.
https://www.youtube.com/watch?v=Qkwp7B
bueqY.

Speakman, Kimberlee. "Oklahoma Schools Are
Now Required to Teach the Bible and Ten
Commandments." *People Magazine*, July 2,
2024.
https://people.com/oklahoma-schools-requir

ed-teach-bible-ten-commandments-8671175.

Stanton, Zack. "How the 'Culture War' Could Break Democracy." POLITICO, May 20, 2021. https://www.politico.com/news/magazine/2021/05/20/culture-war-politics-2021-democracy-analysis-489900.

Superville, Darlene, Tim Sullivan, and Aaron Morrison. "Trump Threatens Military Force against Protesters Nationwide." AP News, June 2, 2020. https://apnews.com/article/mo-state-wire-in-state-wire-mi-state-wire-election-2020-virus-outbreak-a2797b342b4fc509e43f404817a56aa9.

Tevington, Gregory A. Smith, Michael Rotolo and Patricia. "45% of Americans Say U.S. Should Be a 'Christian Nation.'" *Pew Research Center's Religion & Public Life Project* (blog), October 27, 2022. https://www.pewresearch.org/religion/2022/10/27/45-of-americans-say-u-s-should-be-a-christian-nation/.

the Annenberg Public Policy Center. "Americans' Civics Knowledge Drops on First Amendment and Branches of Government | Annenberg." Annenberg School for Communication, University of Pennsylvania, September 13,

2022.
https://www.asc.upenn.edu/news-events/news/americans-civics-knowledge-drops-first-amendment-and-branches-government.

TheRealSnorkel. "Trump Supporters Are Either Incurably Ignorant or Just Plain Evil." Reddit Post. *R/WhitePeopleTwitter*, August 21, 2023.
www.reddit.com/r/WhitePeopleTwitter/comments/15xf580/trump_supporters_are_either_incurably_ignorant_or/.

Van barr, Jeroen M., David J. Halpern, and Feldmanhall Oriel. "Intolerance of Uncertainty Modulates Brain-to-Brain Synchrony during Politically Polarized Perception," May 13, 2021.
https://doi.org/10.1073/pnas.2022491118.

Various Authors. *Holy Bible*. New International Version., n.d.

Walters, Ryan. "Immediate Implementation of Foundational Texts in Curriculum," June 27, 2024.
https://www.documentcloud.org/documents/24780673-immediate-implementation-of-foundational-texts-in-curriculum.

Williford, Anna. "Blurred Lines: What Is Extremism?" *University of Michigan Journal of Law Reform* 52, no. 4 (June 1, 2019): 937–46. https://doi.org/10.36646/mjlr.52.4.blurred.

Wintemute, Garen J., Sonia L. Robinson, Andrew Crawford, Daniel Tancredi, Julia P. Schleimer, Elizabeth A. Tomsich, Paul M. Reeping, Aaron B. Shev, and Veronica A. Pear. "Views of Democracy and Society and Support for Political Violence in the USA: Findings from a Nationally Representative Survey." *Injury Epidemiology* 10, no. 1 (September 29, 2023): 45. https://doi.org/10.1186/s40621-023-00456-3.